The First Vegan on Everest

THE FIRST VEGAN ON EVEREST

By Dr Atanas Skatov

DOLPHIN MARKETING PRESS™

www.dolphinmarketingpress.com

FIRST EBOOK EDITION

Dolphin Marketing Press Ltd Publishing House, 2014

A CIP catalogue record for this book is available from the British Library.
eBook ISBN 978-0-9932452-5-1
Print book ISBN: 978-0-9932452-6-8

Disclaimer

I have tried to recreate events, locales and conversations from my memories of them. In order to maintain their anonymity in some instances, I have changed the names of individuals and places. I may have changed some identifying characteristics and details such as names, physical properties, occupations and places of residence. Any resemblance to real persons, living or dead, events and places are purely coincidental. The views expressed in this book are the author's.

To my parents

Acknowledgements

I would like to offer my sincere gratitude to my parents, Maria and Georgi Stoyanovi, who have supported me throughout all my endeavours, whether they have seen any meaning in them or not, and continue to do so. They are the most wonderful parents. I would also like to thank my sister Nelly and her husband, Johannes Burmeister, who have always helped me with boundless dedication.

TABLE OF CONTENTS

ABOUT THE AUTHOR

ATANAS SKATOV was born on March 11, 1978, in Sliven. He completed his secondary education in his hometown, then obtained a Master's degree in Plant Protection from the Agricultural University in Plovdiv and a PhD from Humboldt University in Berlin.

He has worked as a research associate in Bulgaria and Germany, a university lecturer in Sofia and as a manager and project manager in the private sector in Bulgaria and Germany.

Atanas Skatov has not eaten meat since January 2007. At the beginning of 2012, he completely stopped eating animal produce and became vegan. From his school years until the summer of 2010 Atanas had not been actively involved in sports.

In 2013 and 2014, after becoming vegan, he managed to climb the highest peaks of Africa, Europe, South America, Asia, Australia and Oceania and Antarctica in less than 24 months. He became the first vegan in the world to ever climb Everest.

On October 1, 2015, Atanas Skatov once again became the first vegan to successfully climb Manaslu, the eighth highest peak on the planet at 8165 metres.

Between 2013 and 2019, Atanas Skatov took part in 20 expeditions around the world and successfully climbed peaks. He is the first vegan in the world and the first Bulgarian to have achieved the following:

climbed 11 peaks above 8000 metres, including Everest, on the North and South Faces, 2014, 2017;

- climbed four peaks above 8000 metres in one calendar year in the space of 140 days;
- climbed the Seven Summits of the continents;
- achieved the fastest ascent of two peaks above 8000 metres – Everest and Lhotse, in May 2017, 5 days and 12 hours;
- the first vegan in the world to have climbed to a peak above 8000 metres without the use of oxygen – Cho Yu, 8201 metres, on the 13.05.2018;
- For his environmental work, in June 2018, Atanas Skatov was declared Green Personality of 2019;
- In August 2019, Atanas Skatov received the Gold Medal of Honour from the Mayor of Varna;
- In September 2019, He was awarded the Silver Falcon for Courage and Virility
- Varna sportsman of the year for 2019
- Medal of Honour of the Bulgarian Climbing Union.

ABOUT THE BOOK

The book is a diary of trials and tension, happy and sad moments, and of thoughts and excitement. "The First Vegan on Everest," tells of Dr. Atanas Skatov's preparation and ascent of Mount Everest in 2014, to the Roof of the World. In it, he describes the process of fundraising, the excitement of the trip from Istanbul to China and Nepal, acclimatization in the mountains, his fascinating contacts with Sherpas, the local people and other members of the expedition. All this demonstrate not only how Dr. Atanas Skatov thinks and acts but also how he succeeded in achieving the primary objective of his expedition to prove that a vegan can climb Everest and by doing so popularise veganism.

The First Vegan on Everest. is not just about mountaineering, but about adopting a vegan lifestyle as an alternative to bring about change in people. The abundance of photographic material enhances the documentary nature of the work.

The book is intended not only for lovers of extreme experiences and adventures but also for all those who are in search of a challenge, heightened emotion, and risk, for all those who believe in themselves.

Altitude camps in metres and main points between the last Camp 3 and the summit on the North Face of Everest on the Chinese side

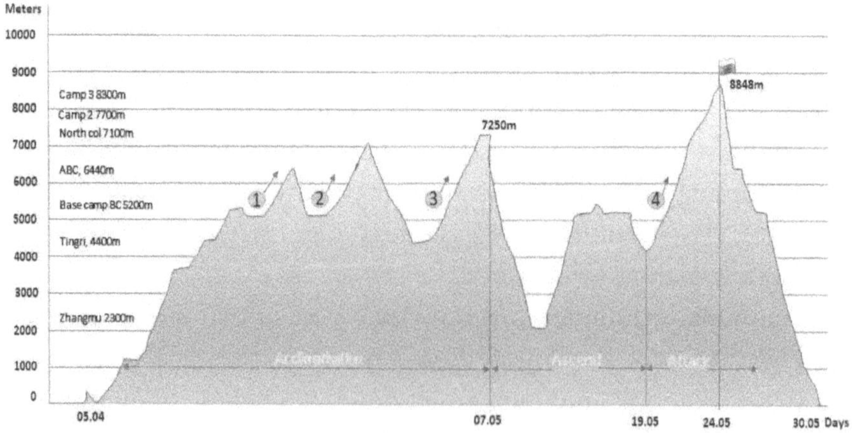

High altitude trek "2014 Vegan Expedition Everest North- Atanas Skatov."

证明书

Certificate

阿塔拉斯 先生 于 2014 年 5 月 24 日 5 时 50 分 在攀登 喜马拉雅 山脉的 珠穆朗玛 峰时 到达海拔 8848.13 米

特此证明

This is to certify that, on 5:50 am at 24th May the Mr. Atanas Skatov has reached the altitude of 8848.13 M above sea level on an expedition to peak Everest of Mount Himalhaya

中华人民共和国西藏自治区登山协会

THE MOUNTAINEERING ASSOCIATION OF TIBET AUTONOMOUS REGION OF THE PEOPLE REPUBLIC OF CHINA

Official certificate certifying the ascent of Everest on May 24, 2014.

INTRODUCTION

IT HAD STARTED SNOWING SOFTLY and there was a light wind. The altitude was about 8450 metres above sea level. My watch showed 23.00, Nepalese time. It had been about an hour and a half since my Sherpa and I had left Camp 3 at 8,300 metres. Although we had set out with the last climbers that evening, we quickly overtook everyone else and acquired a significant lead.

It had snowed softly during the day and there was about four inches of fresh snow. I was in the lead and the Sherpa followed me about two or three metres behind. Earlier in the day, the men from the Chinese Tibetan Mountaineering Organization had set up a guide rope to the peak. They had had to wait for two weeks until the weather was suitable, but they were clearly in a hurry and the guide rope was only set up for about a hundred or so metres.

From Camp 3 the route ascends upwards and slightly to the right along something resembling a channel through alternating steep and slightly more level sections. The visibility is as only as far as your head lamp can shine. We followed the guide rope very closely. We had attached ourselves to it by a Jumara grip which we used to pull ourselves up when necessary. It was very steep in some places and we had to climb on our hands and feet over the snow-covered rocks.

About 20 minutes after a light snow began to fall, we reached a very steep passage at an altitude of about 8500 metres. It was then that the Sherpa shouted to me that the weather was getting worse and we wouldn't be able to reach the top today. He said we had to go back. The snowflakes were very small and the wind was very light. The weather forecast predicted that it would get better after midnight. I objected and told him that I thought the weather at the moment wasn't too bad, and there was no point in standing still or going down. I told him that I thought was should keep going. We had stopped in an extremely unsuitable place. I was holding the Jumara with one hand and my weight was resting on one leg. It was very steep and I had to constantly shift the weight of my body from one leg to another.

The Sherpa radioed the expedition Serdar at Advance Base Camp (FBC) at 6,400 metres and told him that the weather was getting worse and we would have to come down. I also spoke to the Serdar, who told me that the other two members of our expedition, Kristiano and Richard from Poland, were already descending. I was very surprised because Richard was a professional climbing Everest for the fifth time with his client. At the time, I still didn't know the real reason for their refusal to climb. After about half an hour of discussion standing on one leg and hanging on to the guide rope, the Sherpa and I started the walk back down to Camp 3. It was quite obvious that I wasn't going to have another chance because I had started using my oxygen and it wouldn't be enough for a second trek to the top tomorrow.

Everything inside me was crying out that the weather was fine, and I wanted to carry on to the top. I felt extremely strong and in good shape. I felt neither cold nor fear and had no doubt that I would reach the top. We were so far ahead of the others who had set out before us that none of them had caught up, even though we had been standing still for so long. We went down slowly. I followed the Sherpa, wondering what exactly I should do. It made no sense to descend just because of the light snow. I had a thought in the back of my mind that the Sherpas were unreliable, especially above 8,300 metres. I had even heard of many cases of climbers being abandoned by their Sherpas.

After about 10-15 minutes, we reached David from Hungary and his Sherpa from my expedition. It was David's seventh attempt in a row to reach the peak without using artificial oxygen, only with the help of his

Sherpa. He had left Camp 3, three hours ahead of us and could barely move. He looked wretched, exhausted, without an ounce of strength left. However, he wasn't going back. I couldn't believe how hard he was fighting. We stayed with them and talked about the weather. David was in terrible shape, kneeling in the snow and breathing very hard. We took some photographs, or rather the Sherpas took pictures of us as proof that we had reached 8300 metres so that they could get their full pay for getting to the peak. I was still reluctant to go down. At that moment, about ten metres away from us, my Sherpa shone his headlight on the corpse of a climber lying on his stomach upside down and arms outstretched ... he had possibly been there for several years. The Sherpa proudly asked me if I wanted to remain there like the dead climber. The comparison was absurd, given that we had been standing still for the past hour and even started our descent. The temperature was well below zero, and only my down-filled clothes kept me from freezing.

There was another a long discussion, more phone calls, and we headed on down. By now we had lost about 100 metres of altitude and about an hour in time after our first stop. Then I saw the leaders of the next group moving towards us. So I stopped and told the Sherpa that I wasn't going down. I asked him to give me the oxygen bottle he was carrying for me, so that I could go up on my own.

No one could stop me now. I had made my mind up, and there was to be no more discussion. He was quite taken aback and radioed the Serdar again. Then he told me that the Serdar had received a new weather forecast which was more favourable and that we could proceed safely to the top. At that time a group of Russians with their Sherpas caught up with us. We started the ascent again. I led the column of about seven Russians, a Pole and the corresponding number of Sherpas. Tears of excitement welled up in my eyes. I was walking in my own footsteps from my descent. The tears flowed and froze on my cheeks ... It already May 24, the brightest date in the Bulgarian calendar for me!

Between Camp 2 and Camp 3, 8150 metres high, North Ridge of Everest, May 23, 2014, Tibet Province, PRC.

The RongPhu 5000m and Everest

THE STRENGTH OF THE HUMAN SPIRIT KNOWS NO BOUNDS

Why did I undertake this experiment? To dream means to be bold, courageous, fearless, but also sensible and above all to believe in yourself. The difference between having a dream and making that dream come true depends on the strength of your spirit. It depends on how much you believe in yourself, how much you want to make that dream come true, and how much work you're prepared to put into making it happen. This divine Strength of the Spirit moves each of us and humanity as a whole towards new horizons.

For a number of years now, I have been carrying out an experiment on myself. I want to tell you about it here. I won't claim that everything I write here will find supporters. On the contrary, I enjoy criticism and discussions because they bring us closer to the truth. The world is changing every day, in just the same way as we ourselves are changing, and there's no room for extremes in either speech or action.

In early 2012, I began a project, rather a major scientific experiment, involving the ascent of the highest peaks on the seven continents of our planet without consuming animal produce. No such experiment has ever been tried in the world. I wanted to find out for myself whether this diet was suitable for me personally, and if so why not for the entire human race. In a way it was a study of the strength of the spirit, the driving force for achieving inner peace. It was a study of a complete and balanced diet, of sporting culture and physical activity and the natural way of living in general.

In other words, how can a person who has never been actively involved in sport and has no personal coaches, leaders, teachers or experience achieve the desired results.

Besides the highest peaks of the continents, I have climbed many other peaks. I take part in activities to improve my physical and mental condition, and to acquire and maintain the necessary skills and experience for mountain climbing.

THE BEGINNING OR HOW IT ALL STARTED

In 1994, when I was a 10th grade student in Sliven, I heard a story about the longest trekking route in Bulgaria - from Mount Kom on the Serbian border to Cape Emine on the Black Sea, about 700 km with 16,000 metres of positive ascent. Although I had never had any contact with the mountains, I remember being very struck by the idea. I felt that one day I would have to undertake this trek for myself.

That day came 16 years later. In the summer of 2010, I signed up to take part in an organized trek from Kom to Emine together with my father. Or to tell the truth, I signed my father up, to keep me company and we could enjoy the experience of this adventure together. Although we had no mountaineering equipment and even less physical training, we managed to do it in 16 days. Everything I experienced, saw and felt left a lasting impression on me. There were days when it never stopped raining. There were very cold days, very hot days, beautiful views, profound thoughts about life, especially about my life and what I want to achieve, what makes me happy and how I could be useful to humanity.

One day I will write about my first trek from Kom to Emine. I made a resolution that the next year I would once again experience the unforgettably powerful strong feelings, emotions and sensations that come from the contact with the mountains, that feeling of communion with nature, the thoughts, the ideas and the desires that were welling up inside me.

My first trek from Kom to Emine 2010 was my first meaningful contact with the mountains. Before that experience, the last time I had been in the mountains for more than a couple of hours was in 1985, when I went with my mother, sister and father on an organised trek from Buzludzha to Karlovo over Botev Mountain. Sadly, this was our first and last family excursion into the mountains.

I had given up on any physical activity for more than 10 years before this trek.

In 2011, I took the familiar route once again and after that second trek from Kom to Emine, I was convinced that I wanted to dedicate my life to the mountains and all sports related to mountaineering. In the mountains I replete with love, everything was beautiful and gave strength to my body and spirit. Prior to that I had never played any sports, but I delighted in the movements of my body. I loved the way my legs could travel over 30-40 km a day and after a few hours rest, they were ready to go again, as if I was born just to walk.

VEGANISM - IS IT A SUSTAINABLE WAY OF LIFE?

In the summer of 2000, I went to Munich on a summer university course. The main subject was the enlargement of the European Union. One of the lectures was focused on agriculture. The lecturer stressed that the world's population was growing much faster than ever before, and forecasts indicated that by 2020 it would reach 7 billion.

We have already exceeded this figure five years earlier than predicted. There is only limited agricultural land for our food and for the animals we eat. Although in some parts of the world new agricultural land is under development, in others it is being urbanized and its status predominantly changed to industrial and residential purposes. Whatever the situation, there is a limit to the volume of agricultural land. It can't expand indefinitely. However, for as long as there is food to eat, the global population will continue to grow. The greatest part of cultivable agricultural land and pastures is set aside for animal fodder. However, with a reduction in the consumption of meat and animal product, much more land will be available for plant food for humans and thus the population of the earth could double.

So, on the one hand, as an agronomist involved in the production of food for humans, and on the other hand, as someone concerned with the protection of the planet, I started thinking about whether it would be possible to live solely on plant-based food. I don't want to go into the slaughtering and exploitation of animals, environmental and global pollution as a result of industrial animal husbandry. The statistics are catastrophic and no one dares reveal them. Clearly the biggest environmental polluter is animal husbandry which is also the biggest consumer of clean drinking water. There is enough literature on this topic for those who want to read more.

I was very much in love with the mountains and the mountains were in love with me. So I decided to combine mountaineering with an experiment that as yet no one had undertaken. I intended not only to test veganism as a diet, but to find out how it copes with the extreme stresses of mountaineering on the mind and body.

On January 1, 2012, after being a vegetarian for 6 years, I adopted a vegan diet without consuming any food of animal origin. I wanted to see if the human race could exist without animal-based food, since in my opinion we need to experiment to find the optimal solution.

I have been vegan for four years now, and although I still can't draw any in-depth conclusions, I can say that so far I feel great and at this stage I have no intention of changing my diet. I am finding out about new plant-based foods and experimenting by combining them. Doctors say that I haven't been vegan for long enough to make any forecasts about predicting possible future health issues. Some of them are quite pessimistic in their forecasts, but what's more important for me is to see how my body will function in the future. Of course, as I said, all this is an experiment and things may always change. I eat what I like and what I feel like eating. For me, it's very important that everyone eats according to their inner convictions, morals and what they find tasty. Every organism is strictly individual and functions differently in terms of how it absorbs nutrients from food. Over the years, there have been occasions when I've eaten eggs or cheese during an expedition or in the absence of any other food. Every time I do, I get rashes as a consequence which shows me that I am polluting my body with toxins. Once the body is cleansed of them, it reacts sharply even to the minimal amounts of harmful substances contained in animal-based produce.

A lot of people and especially journalists ask me why I became vegan. In the most general terms, it was a long process of physical, mental, spiritual, moral and health metamorphosis. In 2006 I started practicing yoga and found that the consumption of meat and meat products had an adverse affect on my gastrointestinal tract. I immediately stopped, and within a few months, in addition to significantly reducing my weight, I managed to rid myself of a number of health problems. I switched to the almost daily consumption of fish. I still believed at the time that the body needed a certain amount of essential amino acids which are missing in plant-based products.

At the end of 2009, I stopped eating fish and seafood. I can state quite clearly that for me fish is no different from meat, but this is something I only discovered after I stopped eating it. I just no longer needed fish or seafood. I ate cheese, eggs and milk for the same reason - for their amino acids and protein. I wouldn't have believed that one day I would give them up as well.

In the autumn of 2011, I returned to live in my hometown and started walking in the mountains every day. Then from January 1, 2012, I decided to stop consuming all animal products. I didn't know at the time that this was called veganism. After several months I accidentally discovered on the Internet that I had become vegan. I don't know who invented the definition and what were that person's reasons for so doing so, but for the moment I differ slightly from the most common definition of veganism. In addition to the exclusion of animal-based produced, I also exclude honey, and any cosmetics, clothing and anything used in daily life, if it is or animal origin. When I became a vegan, my body still seemed to want to consume a little honey, even though I had barely eaten it in my life previously. I've never really like chocolate and sweets. I don't use cosmetics, and the only clothes of animal origin are my woollen and down clothes I wear when I'm on an expedition. If I could find a company to join me in with my experiment to produce high - altitude equipment without down or wool, I would be a willing participant. I stopped consuming honey in 2015.

My project is an experiment to see whether a person can live without animal products, while exerting him or herself both physically and mentally. There is scientific evidence to suggest that a person can live a full life without eating meat, and even a much healthier one. I don't intend to go deeper into the topic of the harms and benefits of meat. I would prefer that everyone decided for themselves how to live and what to eat. On other hand, we shouldn't wait to fall ill and have to see a doctor or switch to plant-based foods for health reasons.

For me personally, I believe it is extremely important to test the limits of human abilities, and the limits of a vegan diet, since they are directly related to the strength of spirit and belief in unlimited human possibilities. Everything has to take place first in the mind. We first need to believe in it and then put it into practice. I don't want to impose my lifestyle especially veganism on anyone. I prefer for everyone to find their own path to a balanced and harmonious life. My message to everyone is to discover what makes you happy, to find a state of equilibrium between yourself and the environment. Because every dream can come true if you believe in it and invest the right amount of effort. You can't consider yourself as a conservationist, if your eat meat and animal products on a daily basis. The two things are incompatible!

I want to show that there are no impossible things. Everything is possible and everyone should believe in their dreams and in the power of their spirit.

WHY THE MOUNTAINS?

For me, the mountains are something very special. I find everything I need there. In the mountains, I feel free, balanced, at peace with myself. It is a place where I can think about everything that excites or worries me, and find answers to the questions that I ask myself. I believe that the mountains help many people feel good about themselves, not only me. This is why I recommend to those who have not yet felt their magic to just go out and do it. One trek, just a small trek, and if they like it - just keep on going. It may not be your place, everyone needs to find their own. Everyone has their own place on the planet, a place where they feel good, balanced and in harmony with themselves and the environment.

Although mountaineering and mountain sports have relatively recently become part of my life, I am completely dedicated to nature. My aim is for more people to learn that there is another way of life besides that which most of us live. Given that someone who has never really done any sports, and is also a vegan, can cope with some of the greatest physical and mental struggles involved in high-altitude mountaineering, anyone can live life to the full without animal-based products. Behind all this lies the strength of the spirit and the unlimited human possibilities.

The aim of my project is to teach people that the consumption of meat and animal-based products can be easily reduced without impairing physical and mental abilities. There are no impossible things. Everything is achievable if you believe in it and make the necessary effort to achieve it. We need to study our own body and find the best for it while trying our utmost to protect the environment and live in harmony with ourselves and nature. We need to believe in ourselves and the power of our abilities. This is why I set myself the goal of climbing the highest peaks of all the continents on the planet, as well as peaks over eight thousand metres high without consuming animal products.

When I am in the mountains, I feel balanced, calm and replete with love and happiness. The mountains help me discover the most subtle details of my character, and to reflect on life and its laws. I love Bulgaria and its natural environment very much, which is why I was keen to return to live in our homeland.

We have a unique planet, a wonderful place to exist. Unfortunately, with globalization and industrialization, we are increasingly destroying nature and especially its ecosystems. Plant and animal species are disappearing on a daily basis. I feel pain for the planet, and I want what I can now see with my own eyes, what I can smell with my nose, feel with my skin and breathe with my lungs, to continue to exist for our children, grandchildren and great-grandchildren. I want them to have the same chance as us to enjoy the beauty and inspiration of our natural environment. We all need to live in a way which more adapted to the natural environment, and protect our planet from pollution in the most suitable and easily applicable way. We don't have much time left to act. Unless significant changes take place in the way in which we protect our environment, the day will not be far off when we will have realized that we are late.

WHY EVEREST?

My project "Climbing the Seven Highest Peaks on the Continents without consuming food of animal origin" began to take shape in my mind at the end of 2011. At that moment, I was touring the Sliven Balkans and looking for answers from the Force. I had met the mountains the previous year and this was the start of a passionate love affair between us.

In January 2012, I started playing sports and preparing for the peaks of the continents. I dedicated the whole of 2012 to a variety of sports events and competitions and consumed only plant foods. I took part in a number of events, such as: "Speed climbing of the 7 highest peaks in Bulgaria", "In the footsteps of Benkovski", "Aleko" - 100 km walk in 24 hours ", "Zarata" cycle challenge; Kom-Emine trek" for the third time," Cycle Tour of Vitosha", "24-hour mountain bike marathon", "Speed cycling ascent of Cherni Vrah mountain", " Murgash Cycling Cup" and many other sports events. I looked on it as a kind of experiment to see whether it was possible to endure an intense physical load over many hours on a plant-based diet. Don't forget that I had never been actively involved in sports before.

I trained six days a week, took part in competitions and treks in the mountains: Rila, Pirin and Stara Planina. By the end of 2012, I was feeling in great shape, mentally ready, full of energy and willing to get going on my project "Climbing the Highest Peaks of the Seven Continents". At the beginning of 2013, I managed to climb Mount

Uhuru in Africa - 5895 metres, in the Kilimanjaro range, followed by the European peak - Mount Elbrus, 5642 metres in the Caucasus Mountains, combined with my first solo expedition to Lenin Peak in Pamir, Kyrgyzstan. At the end of 2013, I went to Argentina alone to attempt the highest peak in South America - Mount Aconcagua, 6962 metres, in the Andes. My first attempt failed due to very bad weather. I reached 6650 metres, but had to descend and then waited for two days in Mendoza for good weather. At my second attempt, I managed to reach the summit from the park entrance in just 51 hours. My descent from the top to the park exit took another 21 hours, or a total of 72 hours spent in the park—a feat which normally takes two weeks.

A week after I returned to Bulgaria from Argentina, the mayor of Sliven invited me to a press conference to talk about my expedition. One of the reporters there asked me if I was ready for Mount Everest which was also on my programme as the highest peak in Asia. Until that moment no mountaineer from Sliven had ever managed to reach the summit despite several attempts. I had never really given any thought about an attempt on Everest, but I said the first thing that came into my mind.

I answered that I was ready both physically and mentally to leave tomorrow, the only thing stopping me was a matter of finance. So, at the beginning of February 2014, I began to consider the idea of climbing to the roof of our planet in April. I had only two months to raise a significant amount of money. I wasn't worried about my level of fitness, since I had maintained my physical form for the past two years and with each subsequent expedition, I was gaining more stamina and experience. I was fortunate to have had the chance of making one of my dreams come true in 2010. I had already been to Tibet and seen the peak with my own eyes in the autumn of that year when I embarked on a spiritual journey.

During that visit, I had visited the Base Camp on the Chinese side at 5200 metres. Even then, I felt a powerful urge to come back here one day and climb to the top. However, I didn't know enough about the mountains, and the only trek I had accomplished was the Kom-Emine route in Bulgaria a month earlier. At the time, I was in love with mountain trekking and later when I had acquired more experience with mountaineering, this trip to the Himalayas came just at the right time. I discovered that I felt fine at an altitude of over 5000 metres without any symptoms of altitude sickness. There is a reason for everything under the sun. I had never even set foot on Musala before.

In Tibet, they call Mount Everest Chomolungma, which means "Mother Goddess of the Universe." The Tibetan name of the peak dates back thousands of years. I have no idea why the English gave it a different name and now the whole world knows it as Everest, a name which I don't particularly like. This renaming applies not only to Everest, but also to many other peaks in the Himalayas, where the local names have been replaced with Western European ones.

When seen from the North the Mother Goddess is very beautiful, majestic, proud as it rises in solitude above the other eight thousand metre peaks in the area. Even as you travel along the metalled highway from the border with Nepal to the city of Tingri with Mount Cho Oyu to the right, all your attention is focused on the Goddess Mother of the Universe, to the left in the distance.

PREPARING FOR EVEREST

Kutelka Mountain and Golyama Chatalka above Sliven, Stara Planin

AND SO, I ANNOUNCED MY INTENTION to climb Mount Everest, but I lacked the finances. It takes a lot of money to climb this peak not only in comparison with the standard of living in Bulgaria. I already had some experience in fundraising and I knew that it would be very difficult to find someone in Bulgaria prepared to sponsor someone else's ideas. So I began writing letters to all manner of companies, ministries, Sliven municipality and elsewhere hoping to find funding.

After climbing Aconcagua on January 4, 2014, I gave a presentation in my hometown of Sliven in early February, in the aims of inviting business people to get to know me and my activities. After the presentation, almost everyone who came responded to my request for help. The response gave me hope that I might indeed have a chance of getting to Everest. The mayor of Sliven Municipality and the Municipal Council of Sliven also responded and provided me with a significant amount of sponsorship. I had a bit of money set aside from when I was working abroad, as well as a few things I could sell.

As much as it pained me, I had to sell my motorbike, which had given me so much excitement and amazing memories. I even sold my Swiss watch which had been a gift from my sister on the occasion of my PhD graduation in Berlin. It had great sentimental value to me, not just material worth. I rummaged all through my home and advertised everything I didn't need on internet sales sites, so a lot people ended up with my personal effects and clothes. Nevertheless, I needed a lot more money, many times more. I also used social media to spread the word about my project. I found plenty of kind people who liked what I was doing and were prepared to help me in any way they could. A number of Bulgarians living abroad also sent me funds.

During the months of February and March 2014, I managed to keep in shape in the Balkan mountains above Sliven. I trekked and cycled in the mountains. Every morning I did my regular set of exercises which I still do today. The new element in my preparation for Everest was walking with a heavy backpack (more than 20 kg) for three or four hours and a minimum of 1000 metres ascent. It was an exhausting exercise but a very important part of my preparation. At the end of March, I went to Musala and spent four days at the summit for acclimatization and to train in the area.

Up until March 15, I was still unsure whether I was going to be able to leave, and I already had a fixed arrival date in Kathmandu - April 7. I don't know if anyone else has ever planned and succeeded in organising an expedition to Everest in less than a month, but I did. I received enormous support from my parents and sister, who all believed that not only would I get to Kathmandu, but that I would make it to the summit of Everest. This support gave me additional strength and courage. They have always supported me in whatever I have decided to do with my life.

I know that most climbers and mountaineers in Bulgaria viewed my project with a mixture of ridicule and mockery, and that it was too soon for me and that I wasn't sufficiently prepared. I even received some malicious and spiteful letters, but they had no negative effect on me, in fact, quite the contrary. I had a clear goal and target. I was certain that once I set foot on the Base Camp in Tibet, the Goddess would allow me into her white kingdom. I sensed it with my whole being.

The media were not indifferent to my plans and published a number of interviews. They asked why I had chosen Tibet rather than Nepal for my ascent on Everest. Over the past three years, ever since I had seen the summit from Tibet, I had absolutely no interest in Nepal. I was convinced that the only way to reach the summit was through Tibet along the Northern Ridge.

Strange as it may seem, I managed to collect about BGN 25,000 in literally less than a month. Mrs. Stefka Baicheva of "EcoAssorti", a company in Sliven, showed her faith in me, even before I had climbed my first continental peak and offered to help with the financing of my expedition. Another company "Stenata" (Wall) provided me with equipment, and the organic food shop "ImBio" provided me with vegan food. Armeets Insurance Company provided me with insurance cover at their own expense, and medicines were provided to me by a pharmacy in Sliven, whose manager had once been a keen mountaineer. My friend Georgi Balulov provided me with an action video camera to capture the expedition, and my sister sent me her own camera and bought me a plane ticket to Kathmandu. I am also very grateful to "NaviBulgar" and Mr. Alexander Alexandrov. They provided me with a satellite telephone to ensure I remained in contact with my relatives and Bulgaria. Mr. Kaloyan Ganev from "Autobox" helped me not only financially but also organized the logistics for this and all subsequent expeditions.

I found a number of Nepalese companies that organize Everest expeditions from China and chose one of the cheapest. The others were two or three times more expensive. All the expedition companies met the members of their expeditions in Kathmandu, where group visas to Tibet were issued and equipment checked. The distance from Kathmandu to the Base Camp in Tibet is only 280 km, but it ascends 4000 metres, and if you are not acclimatized, you need at least five days to gradually reach the Base Camp at an altitude of 5200 metres.

Three days before leaving for Kathmandu, I met Ivan Temelkov, a climber from Sliven who had taken part in the 2004 Everest North Face national expedition. He was familiar with the route that I had decided to take, and he showed me how to work with a piece of climbing equipment called a Jumara and use a figure of eight rappel, something I had not done before. It's no big deal, anyone of normal intelligence can pick it up quickly, one hour is quite enough. I spent the last two days gathering and packing my luggage. I didn't have much luggage, and I lacked a lot of equipment, but since I didn't have much money, I would have to adjust to the situation. Most of my equipment was second-hand, and when I arrived at the Base Camp, I realized that compared to my colleagues I had almost no equipment.

Trekking in Pirin moutains, 2012

DEPARTURE FROM SLIVEN FOR KATHMANDU AND STAYING IN NEPAL

From day 1 to day 4

Day 1

April 6, 2014

Ataturk Airport in Istanbul

On April 6, 2014, my close friend and sponsor drove me in his car to Istanbul, from where I was due to fly to Kathmandu, the capital of

Nepal. Over the last two years I have been a frequent visitor to this airport and I have flown through Ataturk Airport in Istanbul for all my previous expeditions. The distance from Sliven to Istanbul is only 340 km, in comparison with 310km to Sofia, the capital of Bulgarian, but the prices of ticket from Istanbul are much lower, with less connecting flights. The only problem is the border, and every time I have to cross it, I pray there's no delay so I don't miss the flight. I wouldn't say that we had any problems at the border, except for the fact that we didn't have a green card travel insurance and had to buy it on the spot, where it was much more expensive than in Bulgaria. I remembering saying to myself, I hope that's the only problem.

It's a fast drive after the border, and it was Sunday so there was no traffic. We arrived at the airport a couple of hours before the flight. I had a 150 litre duffel bag, a 65 litre rucksack, and as always I carried my triple-layered high-altitude boots in a separate bag in case I had to put them on at the airport. I had a ticket with Qatar airlines with a connecting flight in Doha and a 13 hour layover. Turkish airlines had a direct flight to Kathmandu, but the ticket was 200 Euros more expensive and out of my budget.

A rest on the way to Istanbul and Turkish tea From day 1 to day 4

I still had several hours before takeoff, and the check-in was not open yet. I wondered whether I would be able to check-in more than my 30 kilograms baggage allowance.

Over the years while I had lived in Germany and travelled frequently, I had learned a trick or two about how to carry more luggage, and I managed to get away with it almost every time. It's true I had a few arguments, but I've never had to leave luggage at the airport or pay for excess. Beggars can't be choosers, but I didn't have the choice.

My hand luggage consisted of 65-litre backpack, which in no way would comply with the rules for hand luggage at all and weighed 18 kg way over the 8 kilograms permitted. I was also carrying food for my layover in Doha and my high-altitude boots. The check-in desk opened three hours before the flight. I took my place in the queue and as always my heart was pounding since I knew I was breaking the rules again, but I didn't want to pay

$10 per kilogram excess.

My turn came, and I could barely lift the 35-kilogram bag to drop it onto the belt. I looked at the sweet-faced young girl and smiled in the hope she would accept my luggage. She could see that the luggage weighed more than the allowance but said nothing. Then she asked me if I had any hand luggage, and like a little boy caught in the act of doing something naughty, I dragged out my rucksack from under the counter with an even sadder face. She nearly fainted when she saw it. I put it on the belt and the scales showed 18 kilograms. The girl stared in disbelief and said that their company had rules. The rucksack was too bulky for hand luggage and I would have to check it. I felt a knot in my stomach. I tried to reassure her that I had always travelled with it and always taken it on board as hand luggage, but she girl was adamant that she couldn't let me take it on board. She had no idea that my friend was looking after two other bags for me, and I would pick them up after I'd checked in. Then I told her that I didn't have any money and I couldn't pay for excess baggage. The girl laughed and told me she didn't want any money, she just wanted me to give her the rucksack so that she could put in on the belt. Then it was my turn to stare in disbelief that she was going to let me take 50 kg without asking for an excess baggage fee. I thanked her from the bottom of my heart for the kind gesture and asked her if she would let me take some things out of my rucksack that I would need for my layover in Doha - documents, satellite phone, cameras, camera, and some other things. I put them in a plastic bag and handed her my rucksack. A huge weight fell off my shoulders. Why is money always such a problem! If I had enough, I wouldn't have to play the fool! I went back to my friend who had driven me there and told him.

I got my other two bags from him. I repacked my bags and put the high-altitude boots in one bag and the things I took out of my rucksack in the other.

We said our farewells and I went on to passport control and security. There was a really long queue for passport control and security which doubled back on itself a number of times. There were a lot of other Bulgarians in the queue in front of me and after me. Bulgarians always complain about how poor we are, but not too poor that we can't travel.

As I was standing there waiting, a former Bulgarian Minister of Finance of Bulgaria with his wife and child walked past me and I felt like shouting: "Police! Stop thief!" He looked around in all directions as if he was being followed. I didn't talk to any of the Bulgarians in the queue. From what I could hear, everyone was going to different places.

After the checks, I headed to departures for boarding. The previous flight had been delayed and the lounge was full, so they didn't let us in. I had to stand waiting for than an hour until they announced a gate change. I had never flown on Qatar airways before, but I had only heard good things about them. The plane, of course, was one of the biggest and brand new. It was almost full and about four hours later we landed in Doha. The food on the plane was plentiful and excellent. I had booked a vegan menu in advance. Doha is a hub for passengers for the entire world. It was by now midnight and I felt very sleepy. Doha Airport is like a city in itself. It is huge, and has everything you could want, you could even get lost.

My layover was 13 hours and I had all that time to kill. I noticed a queue of people and I was curious. I joined the queue too, it was moving quite fast. They told me that if you had to spend all the night in the airport, the airline offered hotel accommodation at their expense. Goodness me, I said to myself, I'll be able to sleep in a hotel. I handed my boarding pass to the girl at the desk, she checked the computer and told me that since I had bought the cheapest ticket possible, it didn't include the option of sleeping in a hotel in Doha. However, she did tell me that were cubicles with beds in the airport itself and that I could rest for the night there, which is what I did. I found a cubicle and presented my boarding pass. They took a note of my flight so that they knew when to wake me. They gave me a blanket too because their air conditioners are quite powerful. These couches weren't the most comfortable in the world, but I managed to get a few hours sleep.

Day 2

April 7 2014

Taking off from Doha to Kathmandu

The next morning I ate the food I had brought with me from Bulgaria and went for a walk around the airport. I discovered a computer area with free internet. I had been all over the world, but this was the most interesting airport I had ever come across.

Once again we boarded a shiny plane again and reached Kathmandu within about 4 hours. However, due to a raging storm, the plane had to circle over the city for an hour until it was allowed to land. We did three circuits above Kathmandu. There was a moment when I wondered whether we would land at all. I had already flown from this airport in 2010 and didn't have any particularly pleasant memories of it. It was a small, gloomy airport ... and lots of people. Nothing had changed. We had to wait for more than an hour for our bags to be unloaded, it was complete chaos, pushing and shoving. I began to wonder if I would get my luggage at all, since there's always a good chance of losing it when you have a connecting flight. More than an hour had passed and there was still no sign of my luggage. I was starting to get worried again. It had happened to me once before in Germany.

There are only two luggage belts in the whole of Kathmandu airport. No one has any idea when your luggage will appear. It's a tiny airport for such a huge crowd of people and you can barely stand on your own two feet. I eventually caught sight of my rucksack, but how was I going to get to the belt when there were three rows of people in front of me all looking for their bags? I managed to push my way through and grab it off the belt. At least I had found a trolley before they all disappeared. After a while, I saw my other yellow bag and breathed a sigh of relief. There wouldn't be an expedition without any luggage. I loaded everything on the trolley and headed for the exit where I had to wait in another endless queue. They didn't check me.

Outside it was raining, and there was no end of people offering you something - a taxi, a hotel, a man, a woman ... whatever you wanted. Kathmandu is the kingdom of nightlife. I did not see my name on any of the name plates being held up at the exit, although the company said there would be someone to meet me. Then someone asked me if I was Skatov, he obviously recognised me. It was a young boy from the company who greeted me and helped me load my bags into a van and we headed for the centre of Kathmandu. It was all so familiar to me - the chaos, noise and traffic. We soon came to a stop in front of the hotel where I had stayed four years ago. An amazing coincidence and a good sign. I remember being very impressed by the food in this hotel. The rooms were nothing special, but the food was delicious and well presented. They gave me a room and you wouldn't believe it - the same one as four years ago. I asked the young man from the tour company to come and get me in the morning. The beds in Nepal and Tibet are huge and a single bed can sleep two people. The hotel was a bit on the old side, and crying out for renovations, but in comparison to where I was headed, it was absolute luxury.

Day 3

April 8 2014

The next morning, as hungry as a wolf, I headed to the restaurant. To my delight, the breakfast table was abundantly laid with plenty of plant-based food. I filled my plate with a huge variety of delicious fruit and then continued with salads and beans. There was tofu as well to my delight.

While I was having my breakfast, a young lady was brought in by the bellboy. She introduced herself as being from Elizabeth Hawley's agency and wanted to interview me. It was their practice to interview everyone before and after the expedition. These interviews were used to create an important database of ascents on Mount Everest from both sides - Tibet and Nepal. Fortunately she was German and we switched from English to German. It wasn't that we didn't get on well enough in English, but German is my second language after Bulgarian. So I ate and answered her questions.

After a while, another man came and introduced himself as the expedition's Serdar, Mingma Sherpa, and told me that he would be waiting for me in the lobby. The journalist was very kind and we talked about a lot of other things not related to Everest. She was impressed with my diet. She confirmed that so far there was no evidence that Everest had been climbed by a vegan. I asked her about the five Nepalese women who had claimed on their website that they had been on a vegan diet for two weeks and had climbed Everest. However, she was quite adamant that they weren't vegans. I found out the truth about this a few months later when I climbed Mount Vinson Massif in Antarctica. Four of these Nepalese women also took part in this expedition. We were together for two weeks and they ate mainly meat and animal produce throughout. I asked them why they had claimed on their site that they were vegans, and they replied that they had only tried the diet for a week and they really liked the idea, but they couldn't do without meat.

All my equipment laid out for checking in my hotel in Kathmandu

The journalist wished me success and let me finish my plentiful breakfast.

Serdar Mingma (the head of the Sherpas and the expedition) was the same age as me. He was my height but looked a little older, and he boasted to me that he had already been to Mount Everest eight times, as well as to other 8000-metre peaks. He had come to check what equipment I had and what was missing. We went up to my room, and I started showing him. He wasn't very focused and missed a lot of things. He told me that he had his own equipment shop and that I would get what I needed from there. He said it wasn't a good idea to have only one set of crampons, and that I needed a spare pair, as well as another blanket, expedition gloves and a down-filled body suit. I explained to him that I had a down jacket and two pairs of down trousers, but he was very insistent that when the wind blows from the north it would get between the jacket and trousers and I would need a full body suit to make my attempt on the summit.

He explained that if I had been making the attempt from the Nepalese side, there wasn't such a strong wind and I wouldn't need one. He said there were a few other small items I didn't have, and I could get at his shop. So we got on his motorbike and we went to the company's office to meet Dava the manager, with whom I had been in correspondence.

When I got on his bike, I felt sad about my own, which I had had to sell to finance my expedition. But that's life, you lose one thing, you gain another. The office was not far from the hotel and we arrived quickly. There I was greeted by Dava Sherpa, a very intelligent man who looked more Vietnamese than Nepalese. We talked, and I signed a variety of documents for Chinese visa and a permit to climb Everest. The visa they issue is a group visa which doesn't allow you to go anywhere other than Base Camp. He invited me to a celebratory dinner the next evening with the owner of the company which has been in the business of arranging mountaineering expeditions in the Himalayas for thirty years. I also met the other participants in the expedition who were in the office.

There were two Poles, Kristiano and his leader Richard, an American, Billy, who had been to the summit in 2009 from the Nepalese side and had ever since wanted to climb from it from the North, but had failed in recent years. He also held the record for the oldest American on Everest. There were also two Indians whose names I can't recall, as well as a Hungarian, David Klein, who had tried seven or eight times in a row to climb Everest without oxygen and thus become the first Hungarian to do so. There were two Russians on the expedition, but they would come later, directly to Base Camp, after acclimatizing on Annapurna. David was accompanied by his girlfriend and a team of journalists from various media outlets in Hungary. He was being filmed and broadcast constantly. They would be staying with him for two weeks, including five days at Base Camp, and his girlfriend would stay until the end of the expedition.

After the meeting at the company's office, Mingma took me to his shop where his wife was behind the counter. The most important and expensive thing I bought there was the full bodysuit. She showed me a couple of second-hand ones. One was too big and the other was medium, my size. It was a good fit but it had damage from wear and tear. She tried to convince me that it was brand new... but it didn't have any labels. But it doesn't matter, they are deceitful and want to get as much money as they can out of you. First she asked for $800. After two hours of bargaining, we agreed on $400, and we agreed that if I brought it back in good shape, she would give me $200 for it. In a word - $200 rent. We also agreed on the crampons. He gave me a set of brand new ones unopened in a box for $150 and promised to give me $100 back, if I hadn't used them when I returned from the expedition. I was sure that nothing was going to happen to mine, but I took his anyway. Then I chose some double-layered high-altitude gloves, but what I didn't know at the time was the most important thing is to be able to use them with the Jumara ascender.

During the ascent, you use the Jumara constantly to pull yourself up and your gloves need to be small and compact, and the Jumara as big as possible. There was no one to tell me these things before the expedition, so if there's anyone planning on going there, they should take good notice of what I've written and use my experience. I bought some small gloves as well, so that I could wear 3 pairs on top of each other. I listened carefully to the Serdar, he knows what he's talking about, he's been there a hundred times before. I also bought a normal bed mat, although

I carried with me an inflatable one I had bought from Bulgaria. I bought plenty of batteries just in case, as well as some training shoes for the Base Camp. All in all, I ended up spending $800 in the shop, expenses that I hadn't planned on. Still, there was a chance I might get 300 back on my return to Kathmandu.

I knew my way around the centre of Kathmandu well. It wasn't until later that afternoon that I sat down in a street side cafe to eat some delicious vegan food. The next afternoon I had to hand over my luggage for Base Camp. The lorry carrying the main luggage was due to leave one day before us, so we kept what we needed for the five days or so until we reached Base Camp.

That evening I found an internet cafe next to the hotel and emailed my family telling them how I was. I didn't have a laptop, phone or Smartphone. My laptop was too old to bring it with me, and my phone didn't have internet, so I left it. I was the only person on the expedition without a laptop or phone. It was a good thing I had a satellite phone, thanks to NaviBulgar.

Kathmandu, Nepal

Day 4

9 April 2014

Today was a day for rest and taking walks. There were still some things I needed to buy like wet wipes and Dava and I had arranged to buy food especially for me for the expedition. After breakfast Dava took me to a big supermarket, and we started filling the shopping trolley with whatever I wanted. I bought about 2 kg of walnuts, 2 kg of almonds, 2 kg of dates, 2 kg of beans, lentils, chickpeas, peas, about 1kg of cashew, dried figs and apricots. I reckoned that was more or less the amount I needed for fifty days. This was just supplementary food on top of the expedition's main rations, especially for me.

In the afternoon, I packed my luggage and handed over my big bag and two boxes of food. I took a walk around Kathmandu. As I already mentioned, it is a very noisy, and dirty city. The streets are filled with all kinds of animals, everything from cats, dogs, pigs, ducks, geese, and even monkeys. However, the monkeys are wild, not domesticated like the animals listed earlier. I visited a number of stupas in the centre of the city. These are sacred places for local Buddhists where they offer up their prayers to the Power. All stupas have prayer wheels and when you spin them, it's as if the prayer written inside it on special papyrus or on the metal itself has been read. Personally, I was most impressed by the pigeons in the squares and near the stupas. There are so many of them and they always flock together. People bring them food and they eat straight out of their hands. Will we ever love birds like that in Bulgaria? When pigeons will land on our hands and we will feed them?

Another typical feature of the stupas in Kathmandu are the two eyes painted on them. They call them the "Eyes of Truth", "Eyes of the Buddha" or "Lemurian Eyes". There are many legends about them, and a lot has been written about them so I won't go into too much detail. I just want to mention one of the legends which says that most of the great stupas in Kathmandu are entrances to caves, and in these caves there are people and other beings in the state of somadhi or samadhi. I have visited almost all the major stupas in Kathmandu and I like the atmosphere in and around them. They are centres of energy for sure.

Kathmandu, Nepal

Stupa in Kathmandu

Swayambhunat Stupa, Kathmandu, Nepal

In Kathmandu

You can buy everything you need on the streets of Kathmandu - all kinds of food, fruit, juice, and when it gets dark, the dealers come out on to the streets. Everyone dozen metres or so there's someone offers you all manner of illegal things: a woman, a man, all kinds drugs and entertainment. You can find copies of original clothes, equipment and accessories. There are also original shops, but they are only second hand or old collections. In the very centre where most of the visitors are tourists, you can find all manner of items related to religion, as well as souvenirs for tourists. The centre is also frequented by men in orange clothes, whose faces are smeared with paint. They go from shop to shop begging or taking pictures with tourists, also for money. I learned that what they were doing had something to do with religion, but I never really found out what.

That evening we all went to a dinner organized by the company. We met the owner, a nice smiling and cheerful man of about 60. They took us to a very interesting restaurant with a beautiful summer garden lit by a huge amount of candles. Sitting next to us were the participants in the Cho Oyu expedition also arranged by our company. Everyone ordered whatever they wanted. The two cooks, Dava, Mingma and other people from the company's office were also present. The dinner went on for a long time because the food took a long time to prepare, but on the other hand, it was extremely delicious. After the restaurant, we were taken back to our hotels for our last night in Kathmandu.

The night before I arrived in Kathmandu, I had a strange dream. I recall it very vividly. I was out hunting or on safari with my father. There were a lot of animals in the distance, including cows, lions, leopards, antelopes and others. At that very same moment, I raised my rifle with its telescopic sight and aimed at the lioness. The lioness fell. I was overcome by a strange sensation. I don't want to kill animals, but I killed her. I aim at another animal, but I decide not to shoot it. I take aim at a target and hit the bull's-eye. My father is by my side all the time.

I don't know the meaning of this dream, but time will tell. After all, it's just a dream. I hunted for many years, not because I liked hunting personally, but because my father would take me along. I wouldn't say that it was a regular occurrence, in fact it happened quite rarely. It was my way of being with my father and doing something together with him. I never understood why animals should be killed. I went hunting a few times while I was a student, but quite rarely, two or three trips a year, in the winter. My grandmother always told me that while I had no children of my own, I should not kill animals, and I strictly followed her instructions. Then I went to Germany to study for my doctorate and stopped hunting altogether. When I returned to Bulgaria, I sold my rifle and left the Hunting Society. I saw no point in hunting. In 2010, I gave up this "hobby" completely because I never saw the point of killing defenceless animals in the most bloodthirsty way. Everyone chooses his or her own way of having fun, what gives them pleasure and how to live their life. I won't judge hunters, everyone decides for themselves what they want to do. It just wasn't for me.

The entire Everest 2014 expedition on departure from Tibet

FROM KATHMANDU TO BASE CAMP

From day 5 to day 10

Day 5

April 10, 2014

In the morning we had an appointment for breakfast at 6.00 am, then at 6.30 am to be picked up from the hotel to reach the border on time and spend the night in the first settlement in Tibet, at an altitude of 2000 metres, just after the border. Kathmandu is at about 1300 metres above sea level. The two Poles were staying in my hotel. All the others were in different hotels, depending on their budget.

As always, I was punctual, and at 6.15, I had breakfast and was ready to leave. At 6.20 Richard turned up and I asked him why Kristiano wasn't coming. He told me that he had woken him up but must have fallen asleep again. He eventually came down at 7.00 and we had to wait until 7.30 to leave. Then we picked up all seven Hungarians and the two Indians. And finally, Bill. He was staying in a top of the range five-star hotel. The owner of the company also came to see us off and tie a special traditional religious scarf on us. We hung around for a while longer, taking pictures of each other. Anyone would have thought we were going to climb Mount Everest.

I started chatting to Kristiano, and he told me that he had been given $150,000 from a vegan cosmetics company, Orig***l S***e, to climb the Seven Continental Peaks as a vegan, led by one of Poland's best climbers, Richard Pawlowski. However, Kristiano turned out to be a fake vegan, stuffing his face with meat, eggs, fish, cheese, milk, milk chocolates and other animal foods every day. What is this world like, I wondered? And he had the temerity to tell me that he was vegan, but he still liked to eat everything. He would become a vegan one day, he said, because he liked the idea very much ... Mamma mia ... He and his girlfriend even had a website promoting abstinence from animal products. Great achievement, though. That's how a fake vegan got so much money ...It's ridiculous ... Iniquity like that doesn't do anyone any good, but it really makes me livid. I couldn't believe that anyone could lie about such a thing just for the sake of money. Veganism for me is something very special and more than sacred.

The other "victor" (with seven failed attempts to his name) - David the Hungarian, was on his seventh attempt time in a row to climb Everest without oxygen. His sponsor had given him over 100,000 dollars just to pay for the team of journalists accompanying him. God knows how much they had given him personally but he had 500 kilograms of equipment, own tents, devices, tables, chairs, and food. And what was I doing? I was combining both their goals and I had raised barely $15,000. The rest came out of my own funds. I'm vegan and I wanted to do an oxygen-free climb. The news I received from both of them affected me badly. It was so unfair to lie about being vegan and to receive sponsorship based on deceit. I had been unable to raise the amount I needed, at least to buy the equipment I needed, but that was my problem and mine alone. I'm not complaining about that but about how unfair it is to succeed by deceit.

Kristiano led by Richard Pawlowski had climbed all the peaks I had climbed alone last year, plus Mont Blanc and Amadablan. But he had done it with a guide and all this luxury, while I had managed it alone without a guide, using my own my money and as a pure vegan. I couldn't bring a laptop to write to my relatives and send photographs to publish on my page. I felt really frustrated, but on the other hand, this really got my hackles up, and I knew that I would make it to the top. One day, sooner or later, everyone gets what they deserve. I have heard that not only in Bulgaria but all around the world, climbers only go on an expedition if they get one hundred per cent of the money needed for the expedition from sponsors. The only case I know of someone else who had self-funded the expedition like me and sold his own belongings, including his car, was Reinhold Messner who climbed Everest alone without oxygen. I imagine there are many other self-funded climbers, but I'm not familiar with their stories.

Although some may say that I am jealous of the support the others have secured, I only want to explain why I mention all this. The easiest for me is to delete this part; however, I started the entire experiment because I feel that we are all interconnected and on the same boat. I take ownership and change myself and give an example that if we all take ownership, we can make the world a better place for our children. I started from almost nothing and try to play fair every single day with the idea that we all can live in a more harmonious with nature lives. Then when I understood of those dubious practices, unfairness and exploitation of the cause of so many people, I was deeply hurt.

It was 10 am before we headed out for the border. There are no highways in Nepal and so it was a slow drive. There is heavy traffic as well, so the distance of 130 km took 4-5 hours with breaks. All the Sherpas were travelling with us in a minibus and a bus. We stopped to rest twice. The local buses are packed to bursting, there are even people on the roof so tightly packed together that an egg couldn't fall between them. It looks really scary when they clamber like monkeys on all sides of the bus. I don't know if the people on the roof pay anything.

These buses stop for breaks in certain places. So that they passengers don't have to get off, the traders bring them food and water which they sell to them through the windows. It would be impossible for them to get off anyway with the bus bursting like that at the seams. They all seemed to be eating sliced cucumbers smeared with something spicy. They eat very spicy food here, so hot in fact that it's almost poisonous. I like very spicy food as well, but here I have the feeling that they're trying to poison me. They also eat a lot of meat and fish. I asked if there were any vegetarians, but it was something had never heard of here. Why wouldn't you want to eat meat?

Intercity bus

Serving passengers without getting off the bus

The natural scenery on the way was so beautiful with its green lowlands and mountains. There are houses being built everywhere. Right in the middle of the fields, you see houses on three or four floors surrounded by wheat, corn or gardens. Most areas are terraced. Nepal has a population of 27 million and there's clearly not enough land. Most people look poor and struggle to survive. The cars on the roads are old and the buses and lorries look like they're left over from the First World War. The roads are pot-holed, and in some places there aren't any. The level of hygiene is pretty low and there's dirt everywhere. They discard their waste wherever they can, so I feel like I'm in Bulgaria on the rural roads or in the neighbourhoods of certain towns.

At around 2.30 pm we arrived in the border village of Kodari, about 1600 metres above sea level. We had lunch at a local cafe and walked to the border crossing. There was complete chaos at the border. Everyone was carrying their own luggage, walking back and forth. Motor vehicles aren't allowed to cross the border. Nepalese women carry all the loads on their backs. The men stand next to their wives and just watch. Perhaps to give the encouragement to carry even more...that's the only explanation I can think of. Very rarely do you see a man carrying something. If a man doesn't have a wife, he has to work too. A pathetic picture. The poor women must weight no more than 40 kilograms. We waited for about an hour, but because we had arrived late, we were told that we would have to cross the border tomorrow. The lorry with the luggage for Base Camp was waiting to be unloaded and transported by a column of about 30 women. So we returned to the cafe where we had lunch. They had rooms available, so it would be no problem to spend the night there. We walked back. It was about a kilometre from the border. There were plenty of rooms, so we were duly accommodated, and I got a single room. The view of the mountains was amazing. Everything was green and the roar of the raging river down in the valley below could be heard.

There are also hot mineral water springs in Kodari, but I couldn't get to them. It's a little village with only one street and houses on both sides with no sewers or water. Every hundred metres or so on both sides of the street, there are outdoor basins with water coming directly from the mountain. Everyone bathes, washes, gets their water for cooking, drinking and everything else ... I don't know why they don't build basins into their houses to supply themselves with water. There is a lot of water, and there's a slope, thank God, for sewage. I saw women and children bathing in ice-cold water. I don't know what they do in the winter.

After dinner Mingma brought all the mountaineers and Sherpas together for introductions. Everyone said a couple of words about themselves, and then I found out which Sherpa would be with me. He was called Gilgen, 44 years old, well-built, fit and muscular. He had climbed Everest eight times, four times from each side. He didn't speak English, but we weren't there to write poetry. After the introductions, everyone got down to work on their laptops because there was Wi-Fi, while I went to my room to relax and went to bed at the same time as the chickens. According to the schedule, we were due to sleep on the other side of the border, in Tibet. The city is called Zangmu and is several kilometres long at a high a altitude. We had planned to sleep at about 2000 metres above sea level, but here it was 1600.

Street fountains in Kodari with water for drinking, laundry, cooking, bathing and other purposes

DAY 6

April 11 2014

I got up early in the morning with a sore throat which hurt when I swallowed. My throat is my weak spot, and I didn't sleep well.

I lay in my bed all night thinking about how anyone could possibly lie to the world about such an important cause. I mean Kristiano's fake veganism. However, the important thing was that I was here taking part in something I had dreamed of - something which brought warmth to my soul and love to my heart ... Nothing is ever perfect, no matter how much I might want it to be. In principle, I'm a perfectionist and I want everything to be ideal. I want people to be happy, satisfied and for there to be injustice in the world.

At breakfast, I always order something vegan which is extremely difficult in these countries where almost everyone eats meat and animal products. It was a good thing they had soups with spaghetti and vegetables and something like fried doughnuts.

A young girl carrying three backpacks at once, each over 20 kg.

On the border between Kodari and Zangmu

This time we arrived at the border at about 10 o'clock. We had to wait a long time again. Due to the time difference between China and Nepal, the two borders have different working hours. This is pretty pointless since when they're not open simultaneously, no- one can pass. We crossed Friendship Bridge where weren't allowed to take pictures.

We handed over the luggage to the women porters. They are like ants capable of carrying many times their own weight.

We crossed the bridge into China where our luggage was checked. We had to wait there for another hour and a half. I was carrying a satellite phone for which I would have had to pay $1,000, the cost of the license to be able to use it in China.Finally, after several inspections, we set foot on the Tibetan "promised" land.

The bridge of friendship between Nepal and China

By now it was already noon, and according to the schedule, we were due to reach the town of Nyalam at 3700 metres above sea level to spend two nights acclimatizing. On the other side of the border, our partners from the Chinese Tibetan Mountaineering Association were waiting for us. This is the only organisation entitled to serve tourists to Everest and the other peaks. Everything is strictly organized and you have to stick to the rules without any deviation. The route is clearly marked out - where you're going to sleep, eat and what you are entitled to. Additional services are paid for in dollars and are extremely expensive. The general belief is that you've come on an Everest expedition, then you must be a millionaire at least. The Tibetans were waiting for us in two vans and a jeep. The good thing was that the people in the organisation were mainly Tibetans. They know the area well and can withstand high altitudes.

The border town of Zangmu starts right after the crossing point and meanders up into the heavens. There must be at least 500 metres of displacement from the beginning to the end of this city. It is made up of a single street with buildings on both sides. At the very beginning of the city we stopped for lunch at the assigned place. This is where we were supposed to spend the previous night. The lunch was delicious, I ordered tofu for the main course, as well as vegetable soup, rice with vegetables and fried potatoes with the others. In the afternoon we headed to Nyalam.

The road through the canyon is very picturesque. It was foggy, and it was already cold. There were rivers flowing on all sides with turbulent, fast waters ideal for rafting.

Photograph from the bus, before the town of Nyalam, 3700 metres. There is no more vegetation.

There were a few stops for document checks as if we hadn't been checked 20 kilometres previously and we had fallen out of the sky. There's only one road here and nowhere else you can go, but we were still being checked. They checked the lists and passports. Not even a bird could fly through here without being checked. The road carries on upwards.

Less than four years earlier in 2010, I had descended this very same road in the opposite direction - from Tibet to Nepal. It hadn't changed much, but it seemed wider in places and in better condition. I remember at the time being struck by the natural scenery because in Tibet there are no trees, bushes, no greenery, and the further we descended, the greener and more picturesque it became. This time I was travelling in the opposite direction, and with every metre the green vegetation became more sparse, as I approached the eternal snow peaks on both sides of the canyon. It's not a long road, but you have to drive slowly uphill stopping to rest. The more altitude we gained, the less vegetation there was, the colder it 9became until eventually the vegetation completely disappeared.

After about 2-3 hours we arrived in Nyalam, at 3700 metres above sea level. It is a small, military town full of barracks and servicemen. They have large barracks and most of the people walking around the town are soldiers. Everyone, of course, is Chinese. It's very easy to distinguish the local Tibetan population. We were put up in a hotel in the centre, and we ate in something like a snack bar, used only in the summer by tourists like us. As always, I went to the cook and started trying to explain to him with my hands and feet that I wanted something to eat something without animal products. I filmed this cook cooking. His cigarette didn't leave his lips, he never washed his hands once, and he cooked the most delicious meals in a very short time. An absolute virtuoso! However, the problem here for me was the lack of protein. The others were stuffing themselves with meat, eggs, cheese, and my arrangement with the company was to have nuts and pulses. No one had called on ahead to say that there was a vegan in the group who needed special food. The rice, spaghetti and potatoes were delicious, and so were salads, but I was used to eating a lot of nuts and getting my protein from them. And I hadn't eaten enough protein in five days. I still didn't know that it wasn't as important as the doctors claimed it was. The only thing that kept me going was the thought that in Base Camp I would find the nuts, beans, and chickpeas I had sent and I could eat whatever I liked.

The town of Nyalam, 3700 metres above sea level

There was an internet room right next to the café. It was like a fox-hole. About 20 computers and as many Chinese playing internet games and everyone smoking like chimneys. I sat at the only free computer to check my mail and send a message telling everyone that I was fine. I couldn't use the satellite phone before Base Camp, because if anyone saw me, they would inform the police and it would be confiscated. So I put two bandannas over my face one on top of the other and managed half an hour in the internet room.

Yaks, dogs, horses, donkeys, cows roamed freely on the street ... The yaks rummaged through the garbage cans looking for something to eat in competition with the dogs. There was one very pathetic yak being chased and barked at by a pack of dogs because it had taken something to eat from a bucket and wanted to eat it alone.

The rooms in the hotel had three beds each. The sheets were damp, plaster falling from the ceiling. We were the first people to come to the hotel this year. The season was just beginning. Two of the journalists accompanying our star David were also accommodated in my room. They filmed him every step he took for the Hungarian press and television. One snored so much I could barely sleep.

The weather here was cool, we were after all at 3700 metres above sea level.

Day 7

12 April 2014

For breakfast there were strange pastries with jam but no fruit, just sugar. Again, there were no nuts, no dried fruit, or any vegan food that I could eat. I didn't feel well and I had a sore throat. I was stiff and my muscles ached. For the past week I had done nothing but travel. The plan today was for acclimatization, but I wondered whether I shouldn't just go upstairs to my room to rest since I had a cold. David had taken the Hungarians off somewhere, and I stayed behind with some of the other members of the expedition and a few Sherpas. I decided that a walk with them would do me good, and I would feel better. There was no way I wanted to go to Base Camp if I was feeling sick. It's 5,200 metres above sea level and it would be more difficult for me to recover.

The 5000-metre snow-covered peaks can be seen from both sides of the town. We started walking along a path which crossed the asphalt road. Gradually we reached a height of about 4000 metres above sea level. It was very cold and windy at this height.

Acclimatisation above Nyalam at 4000 metres.

There were wonderful views of the icy peaks in all directions. We reached a place where there were piles of stones and prayer flags. Other climbers had clearly been here before us to acclimatise. The two Poles decided to climb the nearby peak, but this was enough for me. I began to traverse to return from the other side. Only ten minutes later I saw that everyone was following me, they had clearly given up the idea of going to the top. The wind was very strong and cold and it literally pierced you to the skin. From time to time our feet plunged into the snow. When we started our descent towards the town, we met several yaks. Right above the town of Nyalam, there were three women digging large holes in the ground about a metre in diameter, putting potatoes in them for the winter.

They had either just picked them or bought them from elsewhere. Now they were storing them for the winter in holes with piles of soil on top, so that they would know where they were buried. I imagined that the winter here must be extremely cold.

Nyalam photographed from 4000 metres

Together with the Sherpas

We encountered yaks on the way to the city.

There was a huge hotel being built for people like us on the main street of the Chinese city. They know that the appetite for Tibet and especially for Everest is growing with every year that passes. Apart from Everest, there are two other 8000-metre peaks nearby - Shishapagma and Cho Oyu. Tibet is a magnet for thrill seekers of all kinds - whether by bicycle, motorbike, or car. Some want to learn about the spiritual values of the former Tibetan culture, others want to tour the sacred peak of Kailash. Lhasa is also a very interesting destination. I had dreamed of visiting this country for more than ten years. If someone wants really strongly to achieve something strongly, it can come true. In 2010 I had the opportunity to see something of this country. This time I was in Tibet for another reason, but once again I could reach out and touch this people, their culture and especially the Himalayas!

That evening I was hungry and went to dinner earlier. I wanted to talk to the chef about my food. The manager of the restaurant who was responsible for us was there. He told me he was a vegetarian and invited me to have dinner together. He asked the cook to make us something to eat. We were served special mushrooms with spices, tree ear mushrooms with vegetables, rice with vegetables and a soup. It was delicious, but I didn't know how much protein I had been getting in the last week. I didn't actually know if I needed this protein at all?

I slept for a second night at 3,700 metres and the next day we would be travelling to Tingri at 4,400 metres for another two nights.

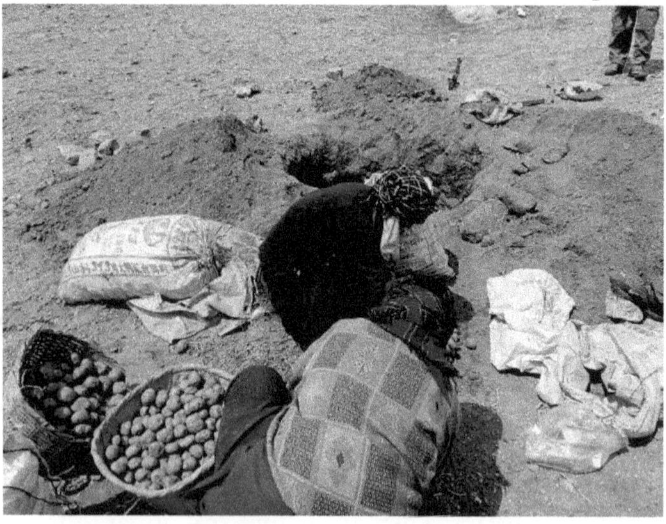

Women digging pits to store potatoes.

Day 8 April 13, 2014

In the morning I felt fine, my throat wasn't hurting any more, but I imagined that one of the fillings in my teeth was chipped. My tooth wasn't aching, but I was worried that it might cause me a problem. Teeth are very important on an expedition, and if anything happened to my teeth, there was no one around to extract it. I just kept telling myself that everything would be fine and there would be no problem. The two nights we spent in the so-called hotel in Nyalam were not very comfortable. The room was very humid during the day. At night the temperature was always 5 degrees. The sheets were damp and plaster was falling from the ceiling. There was no hot water, of course, and there was barely enough water for the toilet. But it didn't matter. There wouldn't be any water in Base Camp either. Despite the bright morning sun, it was very extremely cold. Then I realised that I was missing a thin jacket. I knew very well that I needed it, but I didn't have 400 Bulgarian levs spare to buy one. I had left Bulgaria with a single thick Bulgarian down-filled jacket which weighs a kilogram and a half and is suitable for very cold weather. I knew it wouldn't be a problem to get to the top. I would make it. Climbers 100 years ago didn't have five sets of down-filled jackets, especially Mallory 90 years ago? I think he was the first to climb the top on the route that I now planned to climb. According to our present-day understanding, he had the most inappropriate equipment for the climb. So onward and upward, nothing can stop me now. That's what I kept repeating to myself every day.

I went to breakfast early. There were groups from different companies in the restaurant and we ate in shifts. My group wasn't there and I felt a little tense. One was supposed to be vegan, the other supposedly was climbing without oxygen ... while I was both vegan and climbing without oxygen. The Hungarian journalists who had all been paid $10,000 per person to come to Tibet by the sponsoring company had his sights set on me. The mere thought that I could climb without oxygen and that their man might fail in his seventh attempt was just too difficult for them to cope with.

David was a strange man and barely spoke a word. It was obvious to me that since he had failed six times already, the chance of him succeeding a seventh time was very minimal, close to zero. And there were other things about him that I didn't yet know. He was constantly being filmed with two cameras. He was giving interviews every couple of hours - about him sitting down in the restaurant and then about what he's eating. Such a show. He bought a local hat and a yamurluk and paraded around like a circus act. Most important of all was to have something entertaining to show off about. At breakfast, I sat down with a group of Swiss and Germans who were going to Shishapangma. They were very pleasant people and were very happy that I was Bulgarian and could speak their language. They even gave me some of their own food, because the breakfast was very poor, only fried dough buns with jam, the same jam without any fruit.

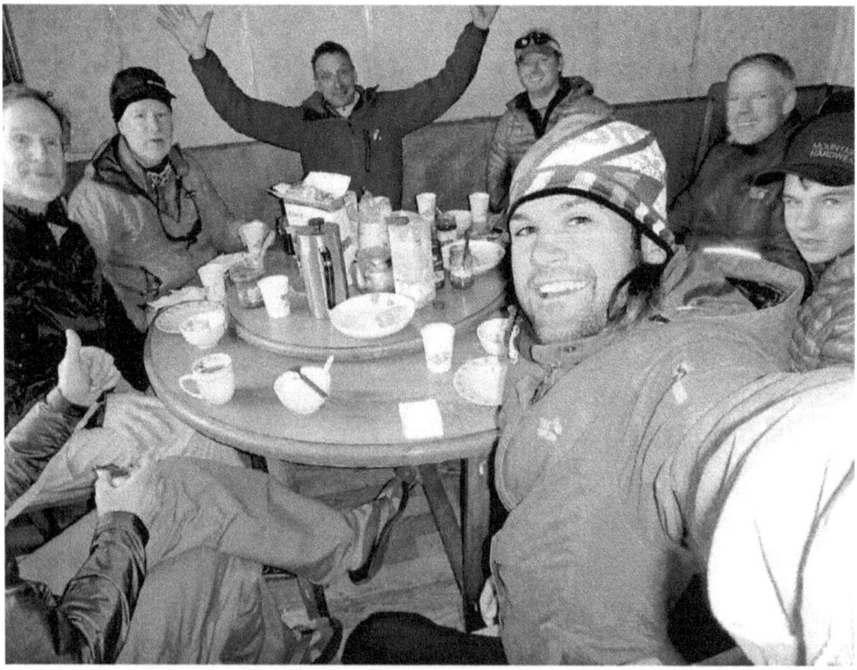

Having breakfast with German-speaking tourists

We had arranged to leave at 9.30 after for breakfast for Tingri. We loaded our luggage into the van, we all got in too, but Kristiano was missing. They went to look for him, and he was sitting in the internet room sending photos and reports to his sponsors. He told us he needed another hour to finish what he was doing. This really got my back up this time. How could he hold up a whole van full of people just because he'd been given a sack full of money and had to be reported in every day? The Serdar decided that we would leave in the van, and the Sherpas in the jeep would wait for him to finish. One of the Sherpas got in the van with us and we headed for the town of Tingri.

On the way from Nyalam to Tingri, before the pass

There is also a large police station on the way out of Nyalam, and they checked our documents there. The road ascends and winds along the river. Further and further upwards. We passed through a variety of villages and local inhabitants. They are small with about 30-40 houses, always built in the same style. The agricultural areas are very small. Only by the side of the river are there terraced areas of land. They have about a dozen or square metres or so where they produce potatoes, wheat, barley and something resembling lentils (dal). People plough with buffalo and reap by hand with scythes. It was a wretched picture. They tended these tiny areas with so much love and cultivated every millimetre of land suitable for production. I felt very sorry for these people whose lives are so incredibly difficult.

The Chinese flag, of course, flies from almost every house. This apparently is compulsory along the central road connecting Nepal with Tingri, and then continues to Lhasa and all the way to Beijing. Every few kilometres there are stone pillars on the roadside indicating how many kilometres are left to Beijing. We were now travelling at an altitude of about 4000 metres above sea level. My only acclimatization was the two nights at 3700 metres, and today we were due to cross a pass 5000 metres above sea level. I wasn't too concerned, since only three months previously I had been at almost seven thousand metres away, so there was still something left of my acclimatization. On the right there were greenhouses between two villages. On the north side they were built of brick while everything else was made of plastic sheeting. Being an agronomist, I wanted to take a closer look at them, but we didn't stop. Next to the road we often saw goats, sheep, and yak. On either side of us rose the tall snow-capped peaks of the mountains.

After about an hour's travelling, we arrived at the pass, at an altitude of 5000 metres. We stopped to rest and take pictures. It was incredibly windy and although the sun was shining it was very cold. My Sherpa Gilgen, the most faithful and very pious of all the Sherpas, had brought prayer flags with him and tied them to every sacred place we stopped. This place was one of the most sacred. I don't know why - whether because it was a mountain pass or for a different reason.

The entire length of the pass was dotted with prayer flags in varying shapes, colour and size. I helped Gilgen unfurl the flags, and then took pictures. The views from the pass are amazing, there was good visibility and the peaks over 6, 7 and 8000 metres could be clearly seen. The 8000 metre peak of Shishapangma could be most clearly seen. Someone else said that Cho Oyu and Chomolungma were visible, but I think they were actually hidden in the clouds. They can be seen in better weather. I was thrilled to be back here again after almost four years enjoying the amazing view of the snow-capped mountains and peaks. These panoramas fill me with energy.

At the pass itself, there were two car loads of local Tibetans drinking buttermilk and gambling. Four years ago, I hadn't noticed how much these people love gambling. Perhaps it was a habit they acquired later. David couldn't pass up the chance of joining in with the locals. He had himself filmed drinking tea sitting on the ground and trying to speak Tibetan. The journalists fell over each other trying to film him. We couldn't stay for too long at the pass, because the wind was too strong and freezing. At the pass itself there was something resembling a fireplace with a chimney. It was used to burn herbs with a strong fragrant aroma. The aroma is something akin to our incense and the meaning is the same. There were snow drifts in places.

The pass at 5000 metres above sea level.

My Sherpa brother Gilgen and me at the pass

The Scenery from the pass, 5000 metres

Prayer flags and a fireplace for burning herbs

We got back into the vehicles and continued on down the road which initially descended back into the lowlands, to about 4400 metres, and then was almost flat. After the descent, the road to Shishapangma forks to the left. It is the only 8,000-metre peak entirely in Tibet, China. Chomolungma, Cho Oyu, K2 and China's other 8,000s are on the border and divided between two countries. My initial plan was to climb Shishapangma to acclimatize and the transfer to Chomolungma as a second peak. However, I didn't have the money... I barely raised enough for Chomolungma. It was almost a miracle that I managed to get things together in the space of a month. After all, the Force had decided so.

We went through another checkpoint where they check your time from the previous checkpoint in Nyalam. If you've been driving too fast, they fine you. At each checkpoint you are given a note of the time you arrived there, and you have a minimum mandatory time to cross to the next. They serve as a sort of speed trap. We had no problems with our time and we were allowed to continue to Tingri. With our group visas for Everest we could only go as far as Tingri, and no further.

We passed through a variety of villages on both sides of the road. There were carts and small tractors laden with goods. We listened to some good Tibetan music in the minibus. I knew most of the songs because four years ago the driver of our jeep had given me a flash drive with Tibetan music and I had listened to it regularly over the years. I felt really at home in Tibet. In one place we passed there was a plant nursery, or something resembling one, where they were trying to produce trees and plant them along the road at an altitude of about 4400-4500 metres. They had tried really hard, and it was obvious that the trees initially grew quite well. However, they stopped growing at a height of two metres and if they didn't die they consisted of a trunk and nothing else.

The Chinese state had done their best to plant trees along the road, and in a couple of places there were small trees arranged in rows to form something like a grove. I thought back to Bulgaria and what a paradise it is with such beautiful and majestic forests. Then I was overcome by a sense of pain and sadness that for the past 25 years the people in government have chopped down all the trees to line their pockets to buy some new yacht or apartment in Dubai. WHY? Why do we want to turn Bulgaria into a desert? Four years ago I had travelled to Israel where I had seen with my own eyes how the Israelis had planted forests in the desert. I saw them trying to plant trees in the rocks and sand and erect irrigation systems over hundreds of kilometres just to create life and vegetation, while we have the most beautiful forests in Europe and we want to turn them into a desert. Something needs to be done if we want our children and grandchildren to see Bulgaria in the way we know it.

Brothers and sisters! We must act now for the forests of the world!

Sitting next to me in the front seat of the van was Richard Pawlowski. He was a well- known Polish climber who had held onto the rope while Kukuczka was dying during his attempt to climb the Southern Face of Lhotse in winter. I was initially very glad to have such a man on the expedition until he revealed his true character.

For the past two years, Richard had been leading Kristiano on his mission to "Climb the Seven Highest Peaks of the Continents as a Vegan" and was paid very handsomely for each expedition. The moment he realised that I was a true vegan and I had climbed the previous peaks all by myself, he couldn't hide his envy. What he disliked most of all was that he could see with his own eyes that their entire mission was based on a huge lie. Richard thought up all sorts of ways to prevent me challenging his client who wanted to be the first vegan on Everest. He tried to play on my mind in all sorts of elementary ways, for example by taunting me that meat is vegan and other stupid and inappropriate statements. He was only too aware that I had seen through their entire project, and that it was just a way of extracting money from sponsors.

However, in a place like this, such primitive human feelings as malice, envy, selfishness, and deceit are secondary, and one concentrates only their own goal and show what they are capable of. I wanted all of us to make it to the top. We had all spent time, nerves and money to come here and fight our way to the summit. If I hadn't been part of this expedition, and if Kristiano had managed to reach the top, then the first ascent of Everest by a vegan would have been a complete lie.

It occurred to me that he wasn't the only one to have abused Everest in the name of money and fame. Like most mountain guides I've met over in the last two years since I've been going on expeditions, Richard looks upon the mountains purely as a way of making money. They only go to the mountains if they're being paid and never without clients. Before I left Bulgaria, I also had a conversation with a famous Bulgarian climber. I decided never to speak to him again. I still can't understand why these people were so hostile, why they felt such malice and envy. I'm just a mountain person, and I feel good when I'm around them.

When the two Russians arrived, I discovered for myself the answers to many questions about Bulgarian mountaineering. One of the Russians had been on the 2004 Russian expedition which had climbed the North Face to the summit. Our professional climbers in the Bulgarian national team financed by the Bulgarian taxpayer had chosen to climb like ordinary trekking tourists with Sherpas, oxygen and all the extras. Later I'll tell you what else Viktor Bobok, the Russian climber, shared with me.

A couple of hours later, there was an incredible view of Cho Oyu and Chomolungma to the right of us. This was about 10-20 kilometres before the city of Tingri. They call it a city, but it's actually more like a village. I had no recollection of staying here four years ago. We were put up in its most modern hotel with private bathrooms and two in a room.

The drivers gambled until lunchtime.

I was with the Bill, the American. He was 72 years old. He looked his age too. I wondered why he needed to come every year and to try and climb to the top. He'd already done it in 2009, but I replied to my own rhetorical question that everyone has to have a dream and follow it. Bill buys permits every year to climb Everest from both sides. His plan this year was to climb both sides in a single season. If he made it to the top from Tibet, then he was going straight to Nepal to try it from that side. Money was clearly no problem, but he too had sponsors and an Internet site. He would report every day to post information about how far he had got and how his expedition was going.

Tingri is 4400 metres above sea level and according to the schedule we would be spending two nights here before Base Camp at 5200 metres.

We were very hungry, but there were other groups waiting and the food was cooked slowly. The drivers and other Tibetans who were waiting, sat outside gambling with dice. I still didn't know that our Sherpas were gambling mad, and for the next two months it would be their main occupation. The annex next to the hotel which served as a dining room is used only in the summer for enthusiasts like us, trekking through the mountains or travelling around Tibet. It had a huge flat-screen TV and the walls were decorated with a variety of Tibetan motifs. There were tourists of different religions and countries sitting at a dozen or so tables. Everyone was waiting for their food. I went to talk to the chef about what they would give me to eat, since I was getting concerned about my protein. Does the body need it as much as the doctors claim, or can we get by with less? Anyway, everything they cooked for me was very tasty. There wasn't a lot of choice. Potatoes, rice and spaghetti for the main course, plus some soup and vegetables. The tofu and the tree ear mushrooms they prepared for me were like a celebration. I had taken to eating larger amounts of carbohydrates to satisfy my hunger. I was constantly hungry and ate a lot. There was always beer, soft drinks or tea. I don't drink beer or carbonated drinks, so I made do with the tea. Lunch was rice as usual, to which you add whatever was on the table: meat, eggs, vegetables, mushrooms, and so on. We were also served with a large plate of fried potatoes.

Tingri is 4400 metres above sea level.

My Tibetan girlfriends having lunch and chatting with me.

I don't normally eat fried food, but here I ate everything, as long as it wasn't of animal origin. After the meal, I decided to take walk around the city which consists of a very long main street with shops, restaurants, hotels, and cafes on either side. On one side of the street there were smaller side streets leading to a small hills with antenna perched on top. I decided to climb it.

The streets in Tingri, like most Tibetan cities, are full of dogs. They walk around undisturbed and compete with the yaks for the restaurant garbage. There's no sewerage here, and the water and everything else from the restaurants and homes flows out onto the streets into special channels. The dogs, cows, goats, sheep and yaks feed near them, and fight often break out between them. I felt most pity for the yaks, some of them looked quite wretched, and they had to fight with the dogs to eat.

First of all I walked down the central street. It was paved in the middle, but there was no asphalt on its sides and huge clouds of dust rose into the air. When I left 45 days later, I noticed that the Chinese had laid concrete pavements on either sides of the asphalt.

Then I turned down some narrow streets towards the hill. I was suddenly approached by a pack of dogs, coming towards me barking. There must have been twenty or more, and I was a little scared. But when

I started throwing stones at them, they ran away. I realized that it wasn't a very good idea to walk around alone so I decided to return to the hotel. However, there were dogs everywhere on the way back too. Then I noticed that they go into the toilets of the houses to eat there as well. The toilets are raised above the ground, leaving a door for the dogs. Now I realised why there were so many dogs. It was their form of sewage treatment. The dogs cleaned up the waste. Revolting.

I barely managed to get back to the main street through the side streets. I went into a shop opposite the hotel to look for a Tibetan hat, because I had forgotten mine in Bulgaria. There wasn't a lot of choice, but I found one I liked and bought it. The shop also had something like a cafe where some of our Sherpas were drinking tea. I joined them and had a cup of tea as well. They were watching a video of Tibetan songs and dances. I asked where I could get hold a disc like it. I really liked their music and dances, and they directly told me that the disc could be mine for 20 yens. I bought it without haggling. Of course, the disk was a copy. There were some Tibetan women in the cafe who were really pleased to see me and wanted to have a look at my hair. After I showed them mine, they took off their headscarves and untied their hair to show me theirs. I took some photographs with them. They were pleasant and good-natured people. Our Sherpas bought lard stuffed in sheep's stomachs. They added it to the soup when we were in the camps.

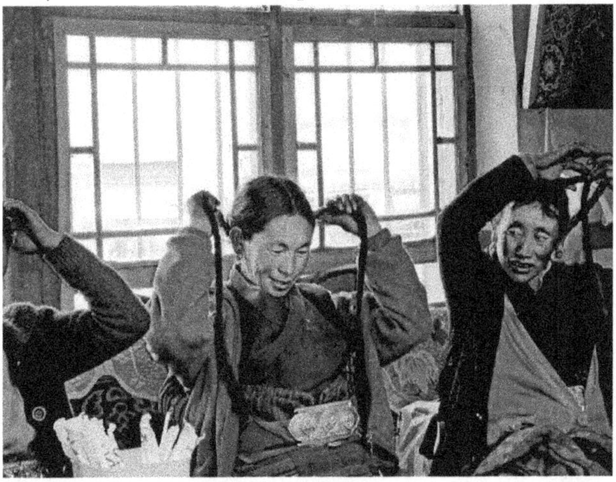

The Tibetan women showed me their hair and how to braid it.

Again, the first thing you notice about Tingri is that it's very dusty and the streets full of dogs. There's no internet room either, not that I needed one. There were nice shops stocked with fruit and vegetables. The prices of the fruit were just like those in the Bulgarian sea resorts in the summer. Very expensive. The people from neighbouring villages come here to do their shopping and sell their own produce.

Nothing special happened that evening. We had dinner in the restaurant again. Almost all the food was meat, and I had only rice with vegetables for dinner. This wasn't veganism, but strict fasting without any protein. That's what I can liken it to. In the evening, Bill turned on his laptop and some other device to watch films, while I went to bed early.

DAY 9

April 14, 2014

The dogs barked all night long. Our room looked out onto the main street. I slept only fitfully. Not an hour passed without me getting up to go to the toilet. I'd been filling myself with water for the past week to acclimatize better. The most important thing is to drink as much water as possible. I drank 5-6 litres every day without sweating. Every half an hour or so I needed to find a toilet. It was quite cold at night in the room. The temperature fell by a couple of degrees. The hotel had solar panels, but because of some problem or other, they wouldn't have hot water until the following week. I had no intention of taking a cold shower and I had missed out on my shower the day before as well. In the morning, when I got up, I did exercises for half an hour to get warm. Then the sun came out and it was very pleasant. The schedule today was for 200-300 metres acclimatisation. At about 25 km from Tingri towards the Nepalese border, from where we had come the previous day, there was a hot mineral bath next to a peak with a displacement of about 300 metres, just enough for acclimatization purposes. After breakfast we packed our bags and hopped in a van to take us there and bring us back.

It was the seventh time that David had been here, and he knew his way around. If we had asked our company to arrange a minibus, the prices would have been exorbitant.

On the unnamed peak above the thermal springs

The path from the mineral springs to the summit

Bill, Kristiano, David, his girlfriend, a Hungarian journalist and I left in the company of one of the Sherpas. It took about half an hour to get to the springs, where there were rooms available and a restaurant. There is one outdoor pool and a smaller one resembling a large bath tub indoors. The water comes straight out of the ground and doesn't have to be diluted with cold water. There are no tiles in the pools, just natural rocks. The water was dirty, but that didn't matter much at 4,400 metres above sea level.

First we climbed to the top. We walked along the path towards the summit where we saw prayer flags. On either side of the path, there were trickling streams of warm mineral water which left marks as white as salt. It wasn't easy going. It was only our fifth day since leaving Kathmandu and we had gained altitude quickly. We walked for perhaps no more than an hour, each at his own pace until we reached our goal. David walked like an old dog in front of the pack and we followed him. At the top there was a fabulous view. We could see Cho Oyu and, of course, Chomolungma, as well as many other known and unknown peaks. We remained there for half an hour and took pictures. There were a lot of clothes left on the top. It is a Tibetan custom to leave your old clothes in places like this to be purified, if there's negative energy accumulated within them. They also leave hair and nail clippings. There were such artefacts here as well. When we had had enough, we descended individually along a different path.

I couldn't wait to soak in the warm water. I love hot mineral water and I can stay in it for hours. On the way down I passed several other springs.

The outdoor pool is larger, but the water in it is quite dirty. They even wash the dishes and food from the restaurant here. No one takes a shower before going in. And there weren't any showers any way.

The outdoor thermal pool

A Tibetan ploughing with yaks near Tingri at 4400 metres altitude

The indoor pool is much smaller, but you have to plug it first to fill it with water. When we returned from the walk, there was about 40 cm of water in the indoor pool which was enough for me. There was a 40-50 cm depression in the middle of the pool which I fit nicely into. I was the only one to take a soak in the water because the others were hungry and decided to eat first. However, the priority for me was water, and I don't like going into water on a full stomach. Having a good soak felt so good! Complete relaxation and tranquillity. I spent maybe an hour enjoying the water and taking pictures with my camera which was provided to me by the company "Drift", along with a range of accessories. Thanks a lot, Georgi! At one point, the Polish climber, Kristiano came in and took some pictures with my camera. Then the others came into the indoor pool because there was a strong wind outside. When I got out of the pool, I ordered spaghetti with vegetables and tofu in the restaurant. I also ate an apple. I enjoyed the meal and hoped that I would come back here again one day.

The driver of the van had been waiting all day for us, but that's what we had paid him for. On the way back, David suggested that we didn't go straight back to Tingri, but in return for a little extra money, he would take us for a drive around the area. We didn't mind, there were plenty of us so it was quite cheap. We drove to a place where there were some old ruins. We saw a man and a woman ploughing with two harnessed oxen, white and black. There was a strong wind was blowing, but then it always does here. We tried to talk to them. The Sherpa said he understood Tibetan. The Sherpa's language is very similar to the Tibetan language. I had read somewhere that the Sherpa caste in Nepal had come from Tibet 200 years ago. There are thirty-two castes in Nepal. After visiting the ruins, we returned to the hotel to take a rest.

For dinner they had prepared three types of salad for me. I was happy, but I hadn't eaten nuts in nine days. I missed the walnuts. This was to be my second and last night in the relative civilization of Tingri.

My dinner in Tingri

Day 10

15 April 2014

The dogs seemed to be barking less and I slept better this night. I felt good, rested and ready for Chomolungma. I felt as excited as a young boy on a first date. There was a knock on the door as if to check if I was there. It turned out that Bill and I, who were in the same room, had overslept and everyone else was waiting for us. I had no idea what time we were due to leave for Base Camp. Breakfast had been at 7.30, and it was already 8.30. No one had told us the previous night what time breakfast would be and when we were leaving.

We got up, packed our bags quickly, but we had to eat something, since the journey's more four hours along a dirt road to Base Camp, about 90km away. There wasn't much left to eat. Just some pastries. We got in the minibus and sped off to Base Camp at 5200 metres above sea level. The dirt road starts directly from Tingri. The fork for Cho Oyu is about 10km down the road. Base Camp is 40 km away, and Everest Base is another 80 km further on. The road is very dusty and nothing but stones and dirt. After about two hours of bumping up and down, we were met by an incredible view of the top. Ah, how beautiful the Goddess is! We stopped to relieve ourselves a couple of time, but I couldn't take my eyes on the top. It was sunny, clear and the visibility was crystal. Richard, as always, was sitting in the front seat to take pictures. Of course, he had to sit in the front since he had only climbed Everest five times, and four times on that side. I was on the back seat in the middle and didn't have very good visibility, only when we got out to take a break. Cho Oyu could be seen very clearly on the right. It was a good thing that I had been to Base Camp four years ago and remembered the way. As we ascended, there was snow in some places.

The road passes through a few villages. All along the road there were flocks of sheep, goats and yaks. I wondered what on earth they found to eat in this wasteland - there was only mosses, lichens and very low and sparse grass. The animals are also very small and thin, but hardy. We reached Rong Pu Monastery in about five hours. It is also the highest monastery in the world. It usually takes about three or four hours from Tingri by jeep, but it was much slower in the minibus. There was another document check just before the monastery.

Just opposite the monastery there is a hotel at 5000 metres above sea level. It was a wonderful day with amazing visibility and beauty. After our documents had been checked, I hoped that we would stop and have a look at the monastery, but we drove on right past it. I was quite surprised, but I would be here for another two months and could always come on foot from Base Camp to visit it. It was maybe about seven or eight kilometres from Base Camp. About three kilometres after monastery is the "T-shop", as everyone calls it. It was short for Tourist Shop. This is as far as you can travel with your own transport. On the military, police and Chinese mountain service are allowed to continue to Base Camp. Everyone else has to get out here but there are buses every twenty minutes that take you to an elevation just before Base

Camp. You get a great view of Everest from here and you can take wonderful photos, if you're luck with the weather. There are a lot of tourists here.

The top of Everest can be seen in the distance all the way from Tingri to the Chinese base camp.

The Goddess Mother of the Universe - Chomolungma, before Base Camp

The T-shop consists of sheds equipped with beds which are rented out to tourists. They offer food, and in front of each shed, there is a stall selling souvenirs and other gadgets. It was exactly the same as it had been in 2010. We didn't stop here either, but continued on for another three or four kilometres to Base Camp, where the mountain service and military officers' administration are located. There's a wide plateau after the viewing site for tourists. It's as flat as a plate and each company has its Everest Base camp here. There's room for at least two hundred more companies. This year, eight companies had set up camps. We were on the far left, next to the Chinese Tibetan Mountaineering Association, which is also the largest company. Although the Chinese had only five clients, they installed the guide ropes and had 60 high-altitude porters working for them. I had no idea how many more support staff they had in the kitchen.

When we arrived at Base Camp, our Sherpas who had left two days ago to pitch their tents and arrange the luggage were already there. There was a food tent for the climbers, another food tent for the Sherpas, a cooking tent, two tents for storage, a tent for a bathroom, a tent for a toilet and another one for telecommunications with solar panels. Everything was ready when we arrived.

One of David's journalists had already left Tingri because of altitude sickness. Four others had paid to stay a total of five nights came to Base Camp. The journalists felt really sick and didn't look like they could manage even three days here. I found a place in one of the tents with the luggage I was carrying with me. Then I went to see the cook and received some very bad news ... I mean very bad news. All the food I had bought with Dava in Kathmandu had been confiscated by the Chinese at the border! The cook had seen the customs officer remove my food from the box. As a plant protection specialist, I knew that there is a ban on transporting plant foods between countries, in order to prevent the transmission of diseases and pests. However, while I was in Kathmandu, I had been reassured that no food had ever been confiscated so far. But now all my food was gone... and I was furious.

I had already been on a strict protein-free fast for the past ten days, and had been eating nothing but rice and spaghetti. Now I would have to survive for another two months on the same diet. Clearly the devil had no other business other than to test how long I would last. Ever since I had left Sliven, I had had to put up with small problems every day, but this today was beyond anything I could have imagined. To top it all, the blanket I had bought in Kathmandu was missing. I had been very stupid not to bring my own cans. If I had had my own can and locked it, like everyone else, nothing would be missing.

Words failed me when the others started getting their basic luggage. They all had their own cans of different sizes and at least 200-300 kg of luggage. David had twenty-five cans and several bags with a total weight of at least 500-600 kg. God, what on earth had I been thinking? I knew that I only had 50kg of equipment and that was far from enough. In addition to the tent provided by the company, David had his own huge tent. It was five by five metres, two metres high with a gas heater. The floor was carpeted with artificial grass. I had no idea what he would use it for, since we had a huge tent for eating in and if you wanted, you could spend all day in it, but he clearly had his reasons. It was after all his seventh Everest expedition. It was such a palaver, solar panels, batteries, two cases of wine, a case of "Johnny Walker", black label - 12 year old whiskey, Havana cigars and who knows what else. He was sponsored by Spa, Austria's largest supermarket chain. They had clearly made sure that both he and his team of journalists were lacking for nothing. The Hungarians wanted to make sure that their man climbed Everest without oxygen, and had clearly invested a lot in him. As far as I knew, he was the only high- altitude climber in Hungary. When I thought about it, my equipment consisted mainly of second hand clothes, a new sleeping bag and some low-quality down clothes made in Bulgaria. The overalls I had were also second hand, bought in Kathmandu. . I had absolutely no idea what else they had in those countless cans and bags. Richard even had 20 issues of Playboy. All I only needed was a thin down-filled jacket, but I knew I could do without it. Whenever I thought I was missing something, I thought of Mallory and his expedition here 90 years ago. I was like a king in comparison to him, and I had no right to complain. What mountaineers they had been then! Now, here they are pampered with their 500kg of whiskey, wine ... and he'd come with a girl to keep him warm.

Chinese base camp

In my new "apartment" under the stars, Base Camp, 5,200 metres.

I had a strange dream the night before. I usually dream a lot every night, but in the morning I don't often remember them. However, this one was imprinted on my mind, and I was even a little scared. Last night in Tingri I had dreamed that my father and I were on a motorcycle, I was driving it. Then a group of foreigners, or rather Roma gypsies, started arguing with us and attacking us. I accelerated very suddenly and the bike flew about three or four metres into the air ... it was very scary because I couldn't get it back onto the ground. Then I woke up. The night before I remember dreaming of the late actor, Chocho Popyordanov. I couldn't remember what it was about exactly, but he was very clear in my dream. I've never met the main in my life. Two days previously, I dreamed that the father of a friend of mine was buying my motor bike which I had to sell to fund my Everest expedition. My friend's father had died ten years previously, but in my dream he was alive and bought my bike. A year ago I had started recording my dreams every day in a file. There were so many of them and I wanted to find some logical pattern about what happens in real life after certain dreams, but I haven't reached any conclusions ... I don't have time to analyze my dreams yet. The dream about the motorbike was very frightening, just lie the dream about the dead man before that.

View from my tent to Mount Everest

The first flag photographed by me ("I love you, Vasko") – Vasko is my son.

The summit of Chomolungma – The First Vegan on Everest.

The entrance to my tent had a view right towards the summit, and I was very happy. When I arrived at Base Camp, I developed an upset stomach. I didn't know if it was the food or something else. Base Camp lavatories are two hundred metres from the tents and consist of two-storey buildings without doors or windows and, like everywhere in Tibet, they have a large opening at the bottom for the animals.

The Base Camp is at 5200 metres and I think we had come here so soon to get used to sleeping at altitude. We had only had four nights' sleep at altitude so far. We should have slept at least two more days at a lower level. Well, it didn't matter anymore, we were here and there was no going back. I was very worried about my missing food. What was I going to I eat for the next 45 days? I was already feeling weak, whether because of the altitude or the lack of protein in my diet. For lunch and dinner there was always rice and spaghetti and everything was cooked separately for me, so that I didn't have to eat any animal produce. I hadn't had enough protein for the past ten days. However, I had no intention of resorting to eggs and cheese for the moment. I couldn't bear the thought of meat. At one point, while I was resting in my tent, I noticed that I had eczema on my knee. My skin had started to peel strangely. Was it an infection from the mineral water the day before, or had my body simply lost a lot of weight? I had been on the roads for ten days and slept in a variety of places with far from clean sheets. I thought it must be from the sheets in the hotels. I had no intention of putting any medicinal cream on it for the moment and I decided to observe it.

ALTITUDE ACCLIMATIZATION

From day 11 – day 32

Day 11

16 April 2014

The first night at Base Camp went well. I hadn't slept in a tent in three months. It was a spacious tent and even had a mattress. During the night there was a very strong wind and I got up several times to drink water and relieve myself accordingly. Over the next couple of months, this was an exercise I would repeat frequently. Drinking plenty of water is one of the most important things you can do to increase the body's resilience to altitude.

Another important thing is to sleep well and eat a balanced diet. You need to monitor yourself and if you have any health problems, seek help or take measures yourself. If you have a headache, nausea, insomnia or loss of appetite, you need to descend immediately to a lower altitude until the symptoms reduce before returning. So far I hadn't experienced any such symptoms, except for diarrhoea, but I hoped it would pass quickly.

Apart from the strong wind, it was sunny and clear. For breakfast there were pancakes (without eggs and milk for me), omelettes for the others, as well as oatmeal, muesli, marmalade, peanut butter, ketchup, tea, biscuits and more. I had brought some hemp seed from Bulgaria and added it to my muesli and oatmeal. In the first few days, there was honey as well. However, it ran out in the first week, because Kristiano was always pouring himself a whole jar in a thermos of tea. The time after breakfast was free, and we could go wherever we wanted. Some went walking, others acclimatized. I decided first to climb the hill I had been to in 2010 from where tourists took photographs of the summit. The wind was so strong, there wasn't a living soul about.

Then I headed north from our camp and started climbing a frozen river. I could have put my crampons on, but I chose to do without them. I climbed slowly and breathed deeply. A good rule for acclimatization is to move slowly and regulate your breathing. I advanced up the frozen river leaving Base Camp behind me. I wondered when I would go to the Intermediate Camp. From my ascents of Aconcagua and Lenin, I knew never to make plans in the mountains. You just follow your natural rhythm and it will lead you. The company that organized the expedition provided us with a sample acclimatization programme for the high-altitude camps.

The frozen river above Base Camp from which we drank water

Base Camp photographed from 5450 metres.

However, it was extremely poorly thought out. According to the programme, we should have gone to the Intermediate Camp at 5800 metres after the third night and sleep there. I kept ascending until I came to a place with prayer flags.

I decided to climb up a steep scree on the right side of the frozen river from which we drank water at Base Camp. At the top, I saw an old roofless building that was once inhabited. It was about 100 metres above sea level sheltered from the wind. There were a few wild goats grazing behind the building and I spent a few happy moments taking pictures of them. The colour of the wild goats was the same as the surrounding scenery, and it was only my keen eye that spotted them 150 metres away. I continued on up for some time to about 5450 metres from where there was a very good view of the all the expedition camps - eight in total number.

Wild goats

Every day lunch was exactly at 13.00 and dinner at 19.00 Although we were in China, we were still keeping Nepalese time because we were on a Nepalese expedition. The time difference was 2 hours and 15 minutes behind Chinese time.

I returned to camp in time for lunch. The cook felt pity for me that my food had been confiscated and gave me a kilo of cashews which I took to my tent. At lunch there was always a first course of vegetable soup, followed by a salad, mostly of leafy vegetables or cabbage. There was always rice served with dal sauce. There was always meat, sausage or fish for the carnivores. The food was delicious and it was a pleasure to eat. The only foods I was missing now were beans and chickpeas. If I still felt hungry, I would eat bread. There was always dessert, compote or fresh fruit. There was no fresh fruit to begin with because the Sherpas seemed to be eating it all. However, after they went up to live in the Advance Base Camp (ABC) at 6,400 metres, we started getting fruit as well. The Sherpa and "members, as the Sherpas called us, always ate in separate tents.

After lunch, I went to bed in the tent. It was very nice and warm. There was a strong wind blowing outside, but inside it was 26-30 degrees, so I washed myself with wet wipes. I hadn't even brought a book to read. I didn't have any way of watching a film like the other climbers. However, I actually liked the fact that I had nothing to read and couldn't watch any films. I wanted to be alone with my thoughts and feelings and to take stock of the past ten days.

My tent was billowing in the wind. Nothing interesting happened until that evening. At dinner I talked to the others for a while, and I could see that the journalists were feeling very bad, as was David's girlfriend. She hadn't eaten in two days and looked as pale as a ghost. She needed to descend. Another journalist had gone back to Nepal ahead of the rest of the group. I was sure that none of them would last the week at Base Camp. One of the female journalists was suffering from a terrible headache and was stuffing herself with all sorts of pills, to no avail. There was only one solution - she needed to descend to Tingri or Kathmandu. Perhaps they would feel better after a second night.

After dinner I went out to look at the stars, they were so many of them - so bright and so huge. A beautiful sky in a wondrous place ...What more does a person need? It had been my dream to come back here and climb to the top, and now I was on the verge of making it come true. I was filled so much love, joy, happiness and boundless strong emotions.

Day 12

17 April 2014

This morning the wind was very strong again. The second night at Base Camp had gone well. The temperature at 21.00 in the evening was 2-3 degrees, gradually falling to minus 5 and minus 10 degrees at about 4-5 o'clock in the morning. It was much warmer in my sleeping bag and I felt completely comfortable. I've never actually liked the cold, even though no one believes me.

When I was a child, I spent three years in Libya, one of the hottest places on the planet. I don't know if that's the reason or whether it's more innate, but ever since I was a child I've loved the heat. In Sliven we often heated our home up to 30 degrees in the winter. The first time I had gone to the mountains three years ago, was also the first time I had skied. Until then, snow and ice had been almost taboo. I wouldn't say that there's much snow in Sliven, but I had never really liked it - not until I sensed the magic of the mountain and got to know it in all its varieties. Now I love walking in the snow. I can spend all day climbing icy slopes and sleeping during the in a tent in the snow. There is a time for everything!

I got up around 7 in the morning, so I could prepare in peace for breakfast at 8 o'clock. Sunrise was around 7.30 and within ten minutes it became very warm and pleasant inside the tent. We vegans have another problem. It's not a major problem, but here, at such an altitude, it could be. When your diet consists solely of large quantities of plant foods, you find yourself going to the lavatory more often, since plant foods pass through the digestive tract several times faster than animal foods. Normally, this happens two or three times a day. And here the food they cooked for us was always quite spicy which significantly accelerated this process. Why was this such a problem? Well, if you have to go to the toilet during the night at minus 5 or minus 10 degrees, you have to put on your thickest clothes so you don't lose any body heat. You have to put on your shoes on, go out of the tent in your thick clothes and walk 200 metres to the toilets that have no doors or windows, hoping that the wind doesn't blow you away. Of course, after that you have to get back to your tent safe and sound, and then get warm again before you fall asleep.

That was my biggest problem on this expedition, especially given my digestive regime.

This morning the journalists looked even worse than the day before. How on earth did they expect to last five more days? David's girlfriend had to descend immediately, but she had been trying to grit her teeth, to avoid embarrassment in front of strangers. She had come here with him two years ago, and managed to make it to ABC at 6400 metres. Now she wanted to reach Camp 1 at 7100 metres. I hoped she would. However, after breakfast, she almost fainted. They gave her an oxygen mask and was rushed to Tingri for resuscitation. I don't know why she'd been forcing herself to struggle for the past three days hungry, thirsty and white as a sheet. She should have descended yesterday. The other three Hungarians seemed to be watching who would last longest. Their transport was due to pick them up from Base Camp on April 22, but they had already seen that every day here was a serious trial for their health.

After breakfast, the Sherpas were due to take us on an acclimatization exercise in the direction I had gone alone yesterday. We were joined by climbers from other expeditions and we walked in single file up the slope. We didn't cross the frozen river that I had traversed, but followed a path.

Base camp, photographed from 5700 metres

When we reached the place with the abandoned building, most of them gave up and went back down. One of our Sherpas led Kristiano and the two Indians up towards a nearby peak. I also went in the same direction. I didn't follow them, I kept a little to the left, considering it a more suitable angle for the top. We walked over some boulders, but the rocks shook and it seemed very dangerous. There was no trail or markings. At one point, I lost sight of the four climbers to my right. I was walking at my modest pace and making slow progress. After about 20 minutes, I saw the Sherpa and my three fellow climbers go back down, because it was becoming very difficult to walk. So far I hadn't experienced any difficulty and continued to move up on my own. The view became more and more beautiful and fascinating, although the wind was piercing. I stopped shortly before the top, where there was already a view of Chomolungma, but the top was in clouds. I poured myself some tea from the thermos and enjoying the amazing view. I was about 5750 metres altitude. Then I went back down.

For lunch there was a delicious meal of flat bread, green beans, or something resembling green beans, a cabbage salad and a very tasty vegetable stew. For dessert there was pineapple compote.

After lunch I saw that our Sherpas, every single one them were gamblers, playing for money. Especially the Serdar and my Sherpa Gilgen. They were addicted and it was their main occupation all day long. They gambled with everything they could - cards, dice, even drafts.

After the meal, I decided to take a wash. The kitchen provided hot water if you wanted to take a bath or wash, and there is a special bathing tent. I took a "shower" with wet wipes. I had found some on the market in Kathmandu - specially designed for expeditions. Each cloth measures 40 by 40 cm, made of a special material used for rubbing the body. Personal hygiene is very important in a place like this where you have to spend months.

Later, as we sat in the dining tent, we discussed the prices of the expeditions, and I found out that I was the only member of the entire expedition who had paid out my own pocket. Even Bill, the millionaire, had a website for donations. I don't know exactly how much he had collected and how much he had paid for himself, but he had been a top lawyer and businessman in Los Angeles all his life. They clearly thought I must be very stupid for pouring my own money into an endeavour which posed a risk to my life. The most expensive expedition was David's. His sponsor had also paid for six other people to accompany him for two weeks. The base camp permit alone is about $4,000. For comparison, it costs about 15-20 dollars per night to sleep in the T-shop. However, the journalists all had permits to spend the night in the Base Camp.

It snowed before dinner, the first time since we'd come. It turned very cold, dark and a mist descended. Now neither the summit nor any of the neighbouring peaks were visible. At 18.00 an hour before dinner, the gas heater was lit in the dining tent. I really liked this custom and I was always the first to sit by the stove to keep warm. After a while it became quite cosy in the tent and we even opened the door.

Day 13

18 April 2014

The next morning I woke up happy, there was no wind and the sun was caressing my tent. The plan today was to hand over our luggage to be transported by yak to the Advance Base Camp (ABC). However, the yak company said it wouldn't happen before April 19 or 20 at the earliest. I had a good night's sleep. It was my third night at 5200 metres and I was already feeling comfortable at this altitude. Breakfast wasn't anything special. It was a good thing that there was oatmeal and muesli to improve the situation. After breakfast, I gave an interview to a Hungarian journalist who worked for KI-Hungary. I've no idea what happened to this interview. It was a sunny day, slightly windy, which is wonderful for these parts. We decided to go down to the T-shop and from there on foot to Rong Pu Monastery.

The official flag of my expedition against the backdrop of Chomolungma

Chomolungma

View of Chomolungma, taken from Rong Pu Monastery, 5000 metres

Buddha at Rong Pu Monastery

From Base Camp we caught the scheduled bus for four kilometres to the T-shop. The price of the ticket for the wretched bus is about 4-5 dollars, but this is Tibet and foreigners are seen as bottomless money pits. They skin your hide down to the bare bone and would take all your money, if they could. That's their motto. We walked around the stalls and then went to the monastery. It used to be next to the T-shop in the direction of the Base Camp, but it burned down years ago and was rebuilt in its current location.

There's still a monastery on the old site, but it only has one monk left to guard it. I visited it about a month later. It's about one hour's walk from the T-shop to the monastery. I was in a group with Bill, the two Poles, the two Indians, and about 5 or 6 Sherpas. We walked along the river where the yaks carried the luggage from Base to Advance Base Camp. The water was very clear, and there was still snow and ice around it. We were 100 metres away from the monastery when one of the Sherpas received a call to tell him there had just been an accident on the Nepalese side of Everest. Several Sherpas had been killed and others were injured by an avalanche while they were building the guide rope for this season. There was no precise information yet. This affected our Sherpas badly. They didn't know if any of their relatives were among the dead.

I recalled the monastery from 2010, when we took a lot of pictures in front of it against the background of Mount Chomolungma. There's a beautiful view of the top from here. More people lived around it than before. They had built a number of mud brick houses. They made the bricks on the spot from the ground and baked them in the sun. There were prayer mills with prayers written on them in front of the monastery. I respect all religions and I consider they have shared principles. I particularly like Buddhism and its customs. After spinning all the prayer mills and praying for health and the success of the expedition, I entered the monastery. I was with my Sherpa, who, as I have already told you, was the most pious of all the Sherpas. He had bought some prayer flags with him again.

When you enter the monastery, first there is a courtyard

surrounded by buildings. Then you climb some steps to a second door to enter the inner courtyard. At the other end of the courtyard is the main part of the monastery. On the first level there is a large room where services are held, and on the second level, there is another smaller room. There was a group of Chinese people shooting a film in the courtyard of the monastery. There are both monks and nuns in the monastery.

Yaks going to work at the Advance Base Camp

I did not know whether everyone slept in the monastery. We went inside where there was a service in progress. I took off my shoes and knelt before the Force. For me there is a single Force, whatever names the different religions give to it. I believe in it, and I believe in good. I prayed for everything that was in my heart. In the main room, the walls were decorated with mandalas and scenes from the life of the Buddha. A nun gave me something similar to our communion bread with the same significance. It smelled very pleasant and the monks' chanting complemented the atmosphere. There were lighted candles everywhere and there was a very spiritual feeling. I felt very humbled and overcome by a sense of inner equilibrium. My soul was calm. The monks lined up to read scriptures from scrolls. After the room on the lower level, I went to the upper level. There were no monks there, just a large metal statue of Buddha. The whole monastery is made of wood and stone. The steps are made of wood.

To the left of the lower room, there are steps leading to the second floor. Tibetan temples normally have three sets of stairs next to each other. One set is used by the monks, other people use the stairs on the other side, and only the Dalai Lama can use the central staircase. At all other times, it is roped off. I noticed that there were only two sets of stairs here and neither was closed. I have no idea why. The monastery also raises yaks, sheep and goats for their own needs.

We returned to Base Camp on the upper road, which I hadn't been down before. We encountered large herds of yaks going to Base Camp to pick up the luggage of the climbers who wanted to climb to the peak or just to Camp 1 at 7,100 metres. The Swiss and Russian companies had clients who only wanted to reach North Col Camp 1 at 7100 metres. Yaks are very timid animals and must be constantly encouraged to walk. There's always at least one person walking with them to guide them.

There were a lot of deserted monks' cells on this road. Before the Chinese came there were hundreds and even thousands of monks here. Tibet was a highly religious centre, and each family gave at least one son and one daughter to serve in a monastery. When the Chinese came, everything changed. They were "liberated". The Chinese refer to themselves as the "liberators". I don't want to comment on that.

We went back to the T-shop, where we caught the bus and went back to the Base Camp for lunch. The Sherpas who had remained in the camp were outside talking and not gambling. They were talking about the avalanche on the Nepalese side, of course.

Everyone was offering condolences to our Serdar Mingma whose father had died today while he was installing the guide ropes. His father was 60 years old and had worked all his life as a high-altitude porter, until the very end. We also expressed our condolences to him. Other Sherpas had lost nephews, cousins, friends and relatives. So far, 15 people had been reported dead, and the rescue operation was continuing. We were all very sad and upset. The Sherpas in Nepal come from one specific region around Everest Base Camp on the Nepalese side and they all know each other. The climbers who had laptops with them followed the news of the tragedy.

Mingma had to leave for Nepal to bury his father. He left that very afternoon. He said he wouldn't be back because they had special funeral traditions which lasted for 48 days. One of the customs was to shave his head. It was a very delicate situation. Many people had died, and no one knew exactly how many were injured. In the morning, about fifty Sherpas had set out to install the guide ropes. They had been caught up in an avalanche between 6,000 and 7,000 metres. After lunch we just watched the news in the tent. There were photographs of the victims and scenes of a helicopter evacuating the dead and wounded. A list of the dead appeared on the Internet. By the evening, 18 people had been reported dead, three missing and several seriously injured but without life-threatening injuries. That same evening the Nepalese government ordered that the 2014 Everest climbing season be closed on their side.

Nepal had sold 380 permits for 2014, and at least the same number of Sherpas would be on the southern side of Chomolungma. The Chinese normally sell about 150 permits every year for the North Face, but curiously this year they had only issued 80. This year we would be the only climbers to get the chance to reach the Roof of the World. As I have already mentioned, I had never had any doubts about what side to approach the summit from. There was only one route for me and it passed through Tibet. A lot of people think it was a matter of luck that I had chosen Tibet over Nepal. That's not the case. One company even offered me a cheaper price to climb from Nepal, but I flatly refused.

At dinner and afterwards, the main topic was the avalanche and the Sherpas who had died. Of course, I called my family on the satellite phone to reassure them that we were fine. I tried to call them every two or three days because I knew they were very worried about me. I felt it without being told. When I talked to my parents on the phone, I realized that today was Good Friday and that on Sunday it would be Easter day. I had completely forgotten about all these things. Eight years ago to the day, my grandmother had died. She was a saint to me, and I remembered her with all my love. Whenever she comes into my dream, they are always interesting and revealing. I continued to dream every night. Sometimes when people treated me badly, and I knew that if I dreamed about them, something bad would happen, or I would get bad news. And this is exactly what happened this time. It's a rule I don't want to believe in, but the facts speak for themselves.

Kalu, the Base Camp cook also left with Serdar Mingma. He cooked delicious food, and prepared everything separately for me. He did not mix animal and plant foods, for which I was infinitely grateful. Nuri, the cook at the Advance Base Camp at 6,400 metres, took his place until a replacement arrived two or three days later. Kalu was not feeling well, although he had been a camp cook for 20 years. He had a problem with diabetes. There were other Sherpas who also wanted to leave, they were a little scared. It was the first time that so many Sherpas had died all together. However, except the Serdar, none of the other Sherpas left. The expedition on our side of Everest was just beginning.

In comparison with the Nepalese route, there are fewer avalanches here, mainly in North Col. On the other hand, however, there was a lot more wind, in terms of duration, strength and speed. There was almost no day without wind. Constant and unrelenting. The routes on the Nepalese and Tibetan sides differ radically in the last stage. I will return to this topic later.

The remaining Hungarian journalists left today. They didn't last until April 22. If I'd been in their shoes, I would have left on the 16th. And I told them so. I didn't see the point in them remaining at 5,200 metres, in such a poor state of health. One of the journalists was suffering from diarrhoea and couldn't make it to the toilets during the night and left little surprises all around the tents. What else could he have done in the cold and desperation? We wished them all the best as they left and suggested they stick to journalism. They wanted to do a final interview with their climber, but he was still in Tingri with his girlfriend, getting some rest.

Would Hungary have the first oxygen-free climber on the Roof of the World? Only God knew the answer. He had to try, but it was his seventh consecutive attempt ... In the case of K2 I have heard that many people succeed only after the third, fourth or fifth attempt. It all depends on what sort of year it is and who will be responsible for installing the guide ropes to the top. The most important element in attempting the 8000-metre peaks is the guide rope to the top, everything else is luck and good weather. An oxygen-free ascent is an extreme test for the human body. I couldn't understand why he had brought so much alcohol with him for the expedition! I haven't drunk that much in my whole life. I had no idea if it would help him. Perhaps it's a mistake that I don't drink enough alcohol to be supported too. What's important is for everyone to do as he or she thinks fit, to feel good,satisfied, balanced and at peace with themselves, others and especially nature. Because we are part of nature, even if so many people don't understand it.

Day 14

19 April 2014

After four nights at Base Camp. The wind had been blowing hard all night long, and it was very cold. If it weren't for that down-filled sleeping bag, I don't know how I would have survived. I dreamed a lot every night and for some unknown reason most of my dreams were about hunting. I was always hunting and shooting animals. Why was the Goddess sending me such dreams? I had completely given up hunting and I hate killing animals. If I could ban it, I would do it in an instant.

For breakfast, there was flat bread and omelettes as usual. All I had was flat bread with marmalade and made oatmeal with hemp seeds. It was a good thing I had the hemp seed, it saved my life. I would like to express my gratitude to Yavor from ImBio for the food.

After breakfast, the yaks arrived and we had to hand over our luggage for the Advance Base Camp, aka ABC, which is at 6400 metres above sea level. The schedule today was for the Sherpas to go to ABC with the yaks and luggage.

First they go to the Intermediate Camp at 5,800 metres, build a camp, sleep for one night, and then ascend to ABC. From here they don't return to Base Camp again, unless they have to wait for a weather window. The Sherpas normally remain above 6400 metres. I didn't have much luggage to be picked up, just one 150 litre bag. I packed the down-filled overalls I had bought in Kathmandu, the high-altitude boots, as well as some other boots I would use while acclimatizing before Camp 1, a sleeping bag, an ice pick, harness, helmet, some food, a blanket and some other small things. The amount of luggage of my colleagues no longer surprised me. I was surprised by the amount of food they were taking for the high-altitude camps, as well as the small gas cylinders, hotplates, and other cooking equipment that I didn't have. The company had written to me to tell me that my Sherpa would have a gas cooker and that I did not need to bring my own. That was very naive of me. What would I do if something happened to the Sherpa? Now I realized that I should have brought everything and relied on no one but myself. I'm still a beginner when it comes to mountaineering. I've got a lot to learn. I can deal with any situation, I'll always come up with something, but you have to think ahead, and above all, you need experience. I already know what to take and what not to take the next time go on a big expedition.

The Poles handed over two or three cans and sacks, the Indians a little less, like Billy. David was the star of the programme with his cans, cardboard boxes and bags. He had a least 250 kilograms. We were entitled to 50, and each additional kilogram costs ten dollars one way. I don't know how much David's expedition cost him. He's also brought enough solar panels for the Advance Base Camp to power a small power station, huge batteries, a couple of laptops and other equipment. It was unbelievable.

We gathered our luggage in one place where it was weighed and recorded. The leader of the yakmen, as the men in charge of the transport yaks were called, was a rather large man for a Tibetan, who turned up in the latest Toyota jeep, wearing a nice down jacket. He stood out like a donkey among sheep and just shouted at them. He stood there, giving orders. Everyone seemed scared of him. He was in charge of the entire yak business.

Weighing the luggage for the yaks. The leader of the yakmen.

He was the only one to provide yaks for all the companies. Although he was Tibetan, he was ruthless towards his countrymen. I'm sure he can't have been paying them more than a dollar or two, and pocketing the rest with his bosses. Great business with no competition. Later on I'll tell you what prices were charged for transport by the only service permitted to do it from Base Camp to Tingri and the border. No one was allowed to use any other transport. Each piece of luggage was weighed very strictly and recorded. They had an old fashioned set of scales like the sort my grandmother would have used. We had a set like it in Sliven, but someone stole it from the yard after the fall of communism. In Klutsohor, the neighbourhood I grew up in, we weren't accustomed to locking the front gate during the day.

Our expedition had a lot of luggage, even though the Russians had not yet arrived, and two others had given up. There was a Mexican who did not come because his brother died just before the expedition, as well as an American woman who was denied a permit and a visa by the Chinese.

The luggage was ready to be loaded onto the yaks to be taken to 6400 metres altitude.

So there were eight of us left in the Chomolungma Cooperative. The remaining expedition members hung around with the Sherpas and yakmen taking pictures. We had a lot of fun. Sometimes they forgot if they had already weighed a piece of luggage and put it on the scales again. It was utter chaos, and I couldn't keep track of which luggage had been recorded and which didn't, but apparently they had a system. At one point, the leader of the yakmen yelled at them and everyone froze. I didn't understand what had happened, but he was angry. They were all like children around him. It was still the strongest who commanded here. There was a strong wind blowing and despite the sun it was very cold. The business with the luggage continued for two or three hours, and in the end it turned out there weren't that enough yaks for today, so a lot of the luggage remained for the next day.

In the place of Mingma, Kristiano's Sherpa was appointed Serdar. He couldn't really cope with the situation, and apparently did not understand much of the language. Mingma also ran some black market trade with the Chinese who did most of the work for him. It was normal practice for the luggage of the big companies, such as the Seven Summits Club, the Russians and Kobler, the Swiss company, who paid better, to be picked up first. We were last in line with our tiny company. Before noon, the Sherpas picked up the luggage and took the yaks to the Intermediate Camp, 5,800 metres. We were due to take the same route the next day. The other members of our expedition planned to return to Base Camp after an overnight stay at 5,800 metres. I had decided that if I felt well, I would continue up to the Advance Camp at 6,400 metres. In addition to our luggage, there was the company's tents, food, gas, and more equipment for another identical camp. We had prepared over 5,000 kg of luggage to be sent to the Intermediate, Advance Base and the other three high altitude camps. An expedition like this requires some serious work. If there's anyone who thinks all it takes is a tent and enough food to get you from Base Camp to the top, then they're very much mistaken.

For lunch, as usual, I ate a lot of rice with lots of spaghetti and a few vegetables. In the afternoon I decided that it was my day to wash my clothes and bathe.

Every day was very cold, there was a strong wind and the temperature was around zero. When there was sun, it was warm inside the tent, but the moment the sun went down, it got bitingly cold. I don't know how what it would be like higher up, but I felt cold enough here. It really irritated the others that I was vegan and that the cook occasionally cooked special food just for me. The Poles in particular couldn't get over the fact that there was a real vegan in the expedition. Kristiano was supposed to be doing the climb as a vegan, but he ate a couple of eggs just for breakfast, as well as fish, cheese, and milk chocolates every day ... There was a lot of bad tension. Then there were the Indians. You couldn't trust them very much or believe them. I only really got along with Billy and we had meaningful conversations. David seemed to be on another planet and had no idea where he was. He had other ideas about life, obviously. But what as normal, since he'd been a professional climber for more than ten years and that's all he did in life.

Tonight I dreamed of my grandmother Maria, who died on April 20, eight years ago. I dreamed we were in Klutsohor in our kitchen. Next to me was my son Vasko and his mother. I was very surprised to see her in my dream. It was a nice, vivid dream. Vasko was very happy. I said something to my grandmother, but I don't remember what.

I talked to the Sherpas today to see if they knew anyone who had climbed the peak without oxygen. They didn't know anyone personally, but they told me that most oxygen-free ascents were made from the Nepalese side. It was a very rare for someone to do it from Tibet. They said that Nepal was very green, with lots of trees, bushes and that there was perhaps more oxygen than here where there wasn't a single tree. The route to the summit from Nepal is quicker too. The last camp is at 7900 metres below the death zone, while in Tibet the last camp is at 8300. What they said about the oxygen content at the same altitude didn't sound very convincing, but I was more inclined to believe that the camps and the traverse to the summit from Tibet were more important indicators.

Day 15

20 April 2014

The wind howled all night long again, but I had started getting used to it. Freezing wind was quite normal weather here. That morning there was a beautiful view of the summit.

The sun was shining, but it was no more than a degree or two above zero with this wind. After breakfast we packed our bags and all the expedition members, together with the new Serdar left for Intermediate Camp at 5800 metres. The route takes you towards the North Face of Chomolungma and after about an hour or so turns left onto the Rong Pu Glacier.

The First Vegan on Everest.

About half an hour after Base Camp we started our ascent of the glacier which forks left and right. There are a lot of stones, soil, sand, soot on the glacier and the ice is visible only in certain places. Above 5600-5700 metres, the ice is transparent and in many places, when the weather gets warmer, rivers begin to flow. To begin with the path is almost flat and stony with a very gradual incline. The entire path is just rocks and dust. The Yaks caught up with us since they moved faster.

At first we all walked together in a group, until everyone found his own his comfortable pace. The two Indians walked together, like the Poles. Bill walked alone, and so did David and I. On the way we caught up with members of the other expeditions, while others caught up with us. There were quite of lot of people that day on the route to the Intermediate Camp.

After about an hour or so we reached a resting spot, where there was even a garbage collection area. This is the last place where you can see the summit, because from here the route turns left and starts ascending. I took a rest, drank some tea and had something sweet to eat.

To my joy, all the vegan bars I had brought from Bulgaria were still untouched. I was keeping them only for special occasions, like while I was walking. They had given us some bread, an egg and an apple to take with us on the walk. I gave my egg to Kristiano. After a break of about ten minutes, I started on up again.

The path was so well marked and there were so many people, that you couldn't go wrong. However, that was only because there was no snow yet ... After turning left and climbing the steep ridge, we came out onto another flat path. There were so many birds that resembled partridges, feeding on tourist waste and lots of yaks as well. An hour later we reached the Tibetan camp. There were several yaks resting here. The poor animals were so terribly overloaded. The documents said that they could carry a maximum of 40 kg per yak, but I saw yaks loaded with at least 60-70 kg. There was a gas bottle and extra luggage on either flank. The yaks worked only for a couple of months every year on Everest to provide an extra annual income for entire families. A slight descent followed. In several places the path went down to the river which was still frozen, and we walked along it. Sometimes the ice cracked underfoot, but the yaks walked over it, so we were confident that there would be no problem. There was steep scree on either side of the path. From time to time you could hear rocks and boulders slipping. We hoped that they wouldn't come in our direction.

At one point, my rucksack started getting very heavy. The plan was that we were to the Intermediate Camp together with the yaks which would carry out main luggage. But we had handed over our main luggage yesterday, and we were leaving today. I had two sleeping bags, one to sleep in the Base Camp and Intermediate camps, and the other for the Advance and High Altitude camps. In my rucksack today, I was also carrying the Base Camp sleeping bag which weighs 2.2 kilograms. I also had my only warm clothes, a down jacket weighing 1.4 kg, and the backpack itself which when empty weighs 2.6 kg, Then there was my down-filled trousers since I was going to be sleeping at 5800 metres, and the next day I would be walking up to 6400 metres. They also weighed a certain amount as well.

On top of all that I had food, water in two thermos flasks, a first aid kit, two cameras and a video, batteries, chargers, a satellite phone which was as big as an ancient mobile phone, clothes ...There must have been at least 20 kilograms. What with the slow walking as well, my shoulders were beginning to ache. On the other hand, I had been suffering from diarrhoea for two days now and my immunity was weakened. I swore under my breath that there were yaks to carry our luggage and I'd paid through the nose for the expedition, and now I was having to carry it all like a yak myself.

The proper tactic was to have three sleeping bags and allocate them to the first three camps where you sleep the most. That way you don't have to carry a sleeping bag all the time, like I did. Bill was the only one to have three sleeping bags, but it was his fifth Everest expedition. In his tent at base camp, he had a mattress about 40 centimetres thick. It was like a bed. He was also carrying all sorts of equipment to keep himself occupied, over 300 films and books as well.

That morning I had attached the camera to my head, and filmed almost the entire time. The traffic was quite heavy - mainly yaks. I was either following a yak, or a yak was following me. They were very timid and afraid of people. There were very steep, tooth- like peaks to the left and to the right. I imagined the view if you climbed to their top. The higher we went up, the more you could see of the glacier itself. I also started to encounter snow and ice formations like in the Andes around Mount Aconcagua. These snow formations resemble people praying and are called "Horcones".

Some of the yakmen mistreated their animals, throwing stones at them and whipping them. I was very sorry to see the animals struggling up these narrow paths and screes. There are no other animals on the planet capable of working at 6400 metres altitude—another world record.

From time to time I took a break and drank tea or water. The path was seemingly endless

up, down, up, down... rocks followed by snow, then ice, then sand. There was no grass or vegetation. I had grown used to the barren land by now. What I like most about Kilimanjaro, for example, was that we started from the jungle and passed through several climate zones in just two or three days. Here, however, the landscape was nothing but rocks, ice, snow and scree.

After about 5-6 hours I arrived at the Intermediate Camp. The other companies' tents were first, and ours at the back after the last hill. There was a Tibetan who stayed in the Intermediate Camp to meet us and see us off when we slept there until the end of the expedition. He didn't speak a word of any foreign language and just laughed.

Richard and I had an argument this morning, and then again during the trek. He was a quite contentious man, as were the Indians, and the subject of the argument was always the same. The Indians were annoyed that I was going to try to climb oxygen free and that I was vegan.

The Rong Pu Glacier between Base and Intermediate Camp

Rong Pu Lake above the Chinese base camp

They claimed that there weren't any people in India who didn't eat meat and that everything was just to deceive foreigners. They added that the purpose of ashrams was only to get money from Europeans and Americans. Then they starter claiming that it wasn't possible for a vegan to climb Everest. All they talked about was that I wouldn't even be able to get to Camp 1. The Hungarian journalists even suggested that I wouldn't last a few days before I wanted to stuff my face with steak. I took everything as just banter and jealousy.

It was very cold in the Intermediate Camp, so it was a good job I had bought my down- filled clothes. Wretchedly cold. The cook first made us some soup to warm us up, then we ate rice and spaghetti with some vegetables.

In my native Bulgaria it was Easter Sunday, I had almost forgotten. I called my parents, then my sister, but I couldn't get through to her. I was alone like a dog with only strangers around me who were either jealous or just irritated. I was determined to climb to the top, no matter what happened. I just have to be healthy, I kept telling myself.

It was a sunny afternoon and it was two degrees in the tent. I didn't dare think how far the temperature would drop when the sun went down. The rest of my expedition was going back down to Base Camp tomorrow. I was the only one who had decided to go to the Advance Base Camp at 6400 metres. Good night!

The rocks above Intermediate Camp

Day 16

21 April 2008 2014

It was a quiet and peaceful night, but very cold. When I got into my sleeping bag, the sky was very clear and without a single cloud. That evening the temperature in the tent fell to minus 5. During the night it fell to minus 13 degrees Celsius. In the morning, the urine in the bottle was frozen, and I waited for an hour for it to thaw in the sun so I could pour it away. I only had one bottle for that purpose and I needed to take it to the camps with me.

Between the Intermediate and Front Base Camp on the Heracles Highway

It was a very sunny and fresh morning. I had slept wonderfully and felt healthy and strong. The assistant cook surprised me pleasantly by bringing me hot tea in the tent. It was such a nice gesture. For breakfast, there was something resembling pancakes, only made of water and flour, and omelettes. It was a good job there was as much jam and marmalade as you wanted. The others were going back down today and I was the only one going up. I had planned to go alone, but the assistant cook was also going up to Advance Base Camp and suggested that we go together. I agreed because I didn't want to go with anyone else. I felt best by myself and I was used to walking alone in the mountains. I packed my bags but left my sleeping bag in storage there. I had another one at the Advance Camp, so I only took my down-filled clothes and electronics.

After the Intermediate Camp there is a descent to the river where everything's covered in snow and ice, followed by a traverse to the other side of the river and a steep section. This is where the "Heracles

Highway" begins. That's the name it's known by. It's a very picturesque path with ice blocks and formations of the most incredible shapes and sizes. There was just too much to film and take photographs of. It was so beautiful. I occasionally let my companion take pictures of me, but most of the time, he took pictures of his fingers.

I called these ice formations below Mount Everest "Ice Creams".

Throughout the journey we walked on the glacier easily jumping over crevasses when the ice cracked. The fissures weren't as big as those on Mount Lenin where I had been the previous year, but I still had no idea what might appear. With each passing minute, the views became more beautiful and breathtaking. We reached a resting place where there were prayer flags unfurled and we drank tea. There were others like us there and we talked to them for a while. The weather was very sunny and windless, but it was still cold. I was dressed entirely in second-hand clothes bought in the shops in Sliven. Over the years they have done a good job for me and I knew I could count on them.

The path was well trodden by both yaks and men. As we ascended, we began to encounter yaks descending from Advance Camp where they had left their cargo the day before. After spending the night at 6,400 metres, they were now going back down for a new load. We stepped aside to make room for them on the narrow path. The yaks were very timid and if you stood in their way, they tended to scatter. After walking for about two hours we reached an interesting place where there was a tent pitched. It was either a resting place for the yakmen or emergencies. There was a waste collection area as well. However, I don't know if anybody ever did any cleaning here, because the season was just beginning and the rubbish bin was overflowing. We took a second break and ate some of the food we had been given at the Intermediate Camp. I gave my egg to my companion, but it was frozen and unfit to eat.

From here the path descended slightly towards the river, then a crossing to the other side of the slope, followed by some incredible icy passages. I couldn't capture everything with the camera. There were some huge towers of ice resembling swords. I named them "Ice Creams." They really did look like ice cream cones. On either side of all shapes and sizes of ice giants and mountains appeared before us as if competing with each other. It was incredibly beautiful. I felt so happy and filled with love for the whole universe. It was worth coming here for this view alone. I was in no hurry and stopped frequently to admire this unique landscape. The summit of Chomolungma would appear before our eyes from time to time from completely different angles. I felt alive!

Such enormous beauty, a perfect day, a perfect companion - he says nothing and we can't understand each other anyway. We know where we are going and how to get there.

Everest on the northeast face, 6100 metres.

In the realm of ice deities between the Intermediate and Advance base camps

On the way to Advance Base Camp, at about 6250 metres altitude

From time to time I gave him the camera to take pictures of me and we nodded to each other. We continued the ascent through the ice realm, and the Ice Princess was kind enough to let us continue. I had no idea how long we had been walking since it was so beautiful that I didn't want it to end. I still didn't know that in a month's time, when I would be passing here for the eighth time, everything would look so different. Every time was so different.About an hour before we reached the camp, we sat down again to rest and for something to eat. I was excited that I would be sleeping at 6440 metres for the first time in my life. I had slept at 6,100 metres the year before at Mount Lenin, but only for 2 hours before leaving in the morning. This would be my new "record" for sleeping at altitude. I knew everything would be fine. It had already been 11 days since I left Kathmandu and I had acclimatized well.

The Rong Pu Glacier below Mount Everest

Advance base camp, 6440 metres.

At some point in the afternoon we reached the Advance Base Camp, aka ABC. It was a big camp, both long and wide. Every company here has a base camp. Our camp was almost at the top towards the summit, only the Russians were above us. Our Sherpas had arrived the day before with the yaks. They had already unloaded their luggage, and even pitched the tents. They were very surprised to see me and let me have one of their tents. They treated me to tea and biscuits. I put all my luggage in the tent I was going to be using for the next month. It was the same as the tent I had at Base Camp. It was just for me which is very important in these expeditions. You need to have your own personal space. I unpacked my luggage, everything was fine... Not that I had a lot. I would be sleeping comfortably for the first time in my new high altitude sleeping bag designed for minus 22 degrees Celsius and an extreme temperature of minus 45. I already knew that these temperature claims didn't correspond very much to reality, or were made for many hardened Scandinavians or Eskimos. In the most general terms, if the label on the sleeping bag says comfort at zero degrees, then by the time it's fallen to 3-4 degrees I'm already feelings cold. Not to mention the extremes. Of course, it also depends on what you are wearing inside your sleeping bag.

My Sherpa brother Gilgen and I, Advance Base Camp, 6440 metres

That evening, I ate with the Sherpas in the cooking tent because the other shared tents hadn't been pitched yet. I didn't mind eating with them. They are, of course, real carnivores through and through and had brought entire carcasses with them. In the evening it was no colder than at Intermediate Camp. When I went to bed it was about minus 5-6. The procedure here was to take a thermos flask of hot water, as well as a bottle of warm water to keep you warm when you first get into your sleeping bag, when it's still cold. I felt good and happy.

DAY 17

22 April 2014

The first night of my life at an altitude of 6440 metres went very well, and I slept like a baby. Of course it was cold, and when I say that I mean extremely cold. During the night the temperatures dropped to minus 15 degrees. The Doiter sleeping bag kept me very warm and I didn't feel the cold, but when you get up to pee in the night or to drink water, you have to get out of it, and within a couple of seconds you're freezing again. That was German quality. Not that I'm a Germanophile, but if you want something rugged and good quality, you need something German. The tog rating of the sleeping bag was minus 22 degrees Celsius, so I felt perfectly warm. I had bought it especially for Camp 3 at 8300 metres, where I expected it to be the coldest.

Near the Advance Base Camp, 6200 metres

Morning sun over Advance Base Camp, 6440 metres

The yaks earning their living.

Yaks lick snow and ice to quench their thirst.

The morning sun warmed my tent and literally in a few minutes the air inside was a comfortable 5-6 degrees. I was in no hurry to go outside. Today I had decided to go down directly to Base Camp. I was thinking about going a little higher to acclimatize before heading on down, but I decided not to risk it. I felt good and would go down after breakfast. I couldn't make my mind up whether to leave my only down jacket here or carry it up and down with me every time. But the weather was unpredictable, so I decided to take it with me to Base Camp.

For breakfast, Nuri, the Advance Base Camp cook made me something like pancakes, except they were smaller and without eggs. They were delicious with jam and peanut butter. Tea is a must and there is always as much as you want. After breakfast, I agreed with my Sherpa that I would go back down today and that I would come back twice more during the next three weeks of acclimatization. He intended to stay and not go back down to the Base Camp, of course, if the weather remained fine and we didn't have to wait for a weather window.

I packed my bags in the tent, arranged my rucksack, and at about

10.00 headed to Base Camp. It was sunny, but the wind was very cold. As you ascend towards Advance Base Camp, the wind is at your back, and now it was blowing into my face. I walked alone down the path I knew from the day before. Today the views were different. I saw the area from another perspective. I used my camera again to take pictures of the amazing ice towers and figures. I descended quickly and passed other climbers and Sherpas who were also descending. I stopped to drink tea at the rest places we had seen yesterday. There were hundreds of yaks coming up from below, and passing was a little difficult in the steeper places. Despite the sun, it was very cold and there was a strong wind. So I kept my down jacket on until I reached Intermediate Camp.

Yaks in the icy infinity of the Himalayas.

I arrived at the Intermediate Camp in about three hours. There was a Tibetan lad called Sambo whose "punishment" it was to stay there until the end of the expedition. He met us and saw us off. He made me some pancakes to eat and returned the sleeping bag I had left with him the day before. I hoped he hadn't slept in it. Sambo wasn't a cook, but he made simple things like spaghetti, rice, soups, cakes and pancakes. I ate quickly, rested a little, and headed for Base Camp. It wasn't a short journey and my backpack weighed over 15 kilograms. The expedition members usually carry small, light rucksacks. For my sins, I was the only one carrying such a heavy one. I would know the tactics for next time.

The path starts with a steep descent, then alternating ascents and descents, loops around the river, several crossings over both sides of the gorge, as well as traversing the frozen river. There were a lot of yaks climbing that day. When I thought that only 80 permits had been issued by China this year, I couldn't imagine what it would have been like if the normal 150 permits had been sold.

I descended slowly and gloriously, while all the time thinking about my life. I was missing my son Vasko enormously. I hadn't seen him in months, even though I really wanted to. I imagined what a great big boy he must have become. And when I got back, I imagined how we would walk together in the mountains and sleep in a tent. I also felt sorry for my parents who were worrying about me. With these expeditions of mine, all I did was to give them headaches. They never said anything and even encouraged me to do what I wanted most.

It was so quiet, calm and beautiful. I admired the peaks standing proud like skyscrapers up into the sky. There were some ridges on the right around the Tibetan camp. I was met again by the wild hens which wandered past me. I sat down to rest for a while, to have a drink of tea, and recharge my batteries with something sweet.

At about 6 pm, I arrived safe and sound at Base Camp. There I was greeted by the new additions from Russia – Alex, the oligarch, and his guide, Victor Bobok. They had acclimatized in the Annapurna area and arrived yesterday. The others had been here relaxing since yesterday. After dinner, there was a very beautiful sunset, and I photographed the top again. I planned to rest here for at least two days before heading back to Advance Base Camp.

I forgot to mention that today throughout my descent, there had been a very strong wind and I had deviated from the path a couple or three times, but then I quickly found it again. The rucksack was really heavy and I felt absolutely crushed.

DAY 18

April 23 2014

I slept soundly for 12 hours that night. I didn't wake once, not even to drink water or go to the toilet. I was so tired after carrying that rucksack. I was woken by the pleasant sun. The wind was still blowing, but who cared. I had decided to do some laundry today because I hadn't got any clean clothes left. After breakfast the new cook gave me some hot water. I had brought laundry soap from Bulgaria. As I've already mentioned, we had a special small tent for laundry where we could also take a shower.

I felt very well, healthy, rested and well acclimatized. Last night at dinner I chatted to the two new members in the group. Victor, the guide, had climbed Everest four times, including once on a 2004 Russian expedition along the North Face. That same year the Bulgarian team had opted for the pedestrian route rather than climbing one. He had also climbed Vinson Massif four times and no end of other peaks.

He was a professional guide and took people all over the world, especially to all the Seven Summits. Four years ago, he had taken Alexander (his present client) to the Vinson Massif, where they met. Like me, Alex's goal was to climb the highest peaks in the continents, but he's a carnivore and millionaire - in his own words. He boasted that he had homes in London and Moscow and a 35-metre yacht. He had eight bags of luggage. He was an odd type, sometimes with a serious expression on his face, and then looking around like a rabbit in silence. They both carried laptops and were constantly on the internet. Victor, of course, had plenty of vodka.

I asked Victor, as a consummate professional, for his opinion on climbing Everest oxygen- free. I still wanted to try it without oxygen. He told me that the top was full of corpses of people who tried, and that in his opinion it was utter folly. He and his client had six bottles of oxygen each and would be using them from 7,100 metres onwards. Nevertheless, I felt that I could make it without oxygen, but I was worried about the lack of variety in the food. For the past 20 days, my body has been receiving only carbohydrates - rice, potatoes and spaghetti, and I had the same amount of time still to go. I needed beans, chickpeas, peas, fruits, vegetables and nuts. They had promised to bring me some from Tingri, but they didn't do anything about it. That's how it was going to be from now on.

The route from Base to Advanced Base Camp is more than 25 kilometres long, very dusty and my clothes were by now filthy. I hoped there wouldn't be as much dust after the Advance Camp, because it was starting to snow and at least I wouldn't have to wash them. I felt very tired after yesterday, mainly because of my rucksack, and perhaps because I had slept at 6440 metres. I did my laundry and had a sleep in my warm tent in the afternoon.

On the way to the Base Camp, 5400 metres

DAY 19

24 April 2014

I slept like a baby that night. At 5200 metres, I was beginning to feel as if I was at 200. My heart rate was normal. Not that I had any heart rate monitors or blood oxygen metres. Again, I was the only one without such toys. Did Mallory measure his blood oxygen in the morning, at noon, and in the evening? Only once did I ask Bill if I could borrow his "Tamagotchi" to measure my saturation. Victor and the others checked the levels in the morning and evening. Perhaps it helps I don't know. I might get one for myself one day.

There was a strong wind blowing again today, but it didn't bother me anymore. Ten of us sat down to breakfast, and there was barely room at the table. David's girlfriend had returned from Tingri and was feeling better. It was another day of rest for me. I planned to sleep at the Intermediate Camp tomorrow, then at the Advanced Camp. My goal was to go to Camp 1 at 7100 metres in the space of one day, rest for two days at the Advance Camp at 6440 metres, and then climb to 7100 metres again but with an overnight stay. This meant spending 5-6 days over 6440 metres with an overnight stay at 7100 metres. However, these were only plans. What would really happen would be decided only by the Force and in this case - the Mother Goddess.

After breakfast, I took a short walk around the area. I had never visited the other tent camps before. Even though they were only 300-400 metres from ours, I hadn't been to see them. At the far end was the Russian camp made up of huge round tents. They had Persian rugs at their entrances. They were incredibly luxurious, and even had huge plasma TVs. Food and drink fit for a cocktail party constantly available on tables. Beer, whisky, cans of soft drinks. They had one tent for food, another for the internet, they even had a steam bath. The members themselves slept in much larger tents than ours. Some of them had extended entrance corridors and they were made by the best tent company in the world. They'd paid three times more than me, but their conditions were completely different. Their food was no doubt much better as well. Every two or three members had their own guide, in addition to the obligatory Sherpas. It was a serious company with a serious owner who spent all his time with his clients, and climbed to the top with them every year. The site even had artificial landscaping to create a friendly atmosphere. There were about 20 members, and at least 40 staff to take care of them.

The next camp I visited was Kobler's Swiss camp. The members' tents were tall and fitted with beds. They didn't have to bend over a hundred times every day to get in and out, like me in my little tent. I don't know how I would have coped if I was two metres tall. Kobler also had one of those huge spherical tents with Persian rugs inside it. It was also equipped with gas burners, TVs, Internet, and as much drink as you could want — beer, alcohol, and soft drinks. I met a German woman who was there for a third time with Kobler. She was only going to Camp 1 at 7,100 metres to sleep and then go down again. Some people only want to go as far as 7100 metres below the peak of Chomolungma.

View of Chomolungma from my tent

It doesn't do any harm to have a little luxury at 5200 metres, especially when you've got enough problems to deal with every day. For the third day in a row, I was suffering from diarrhoea and the nightly walk to the toilets in the distance was really exhausting. I was taking several different pills every day - vitamins, cordyceps, echinacea, Ginko biloba and various others, to help me adjust to the altitude, as well as to boost my body's immunity. I eventually got tired of taking them like some old grandmother and I just gave them all up. I'd make it to the top with or without them. My stomach sorted itself out when I stopped taking them.

The other colleagues, with the exception of David, left for Intermediate Camp today, so there were only three of us left - me, him, and his girlfriend. David was used to his luxuries. In the evening he wouldn't sit down to dinner without wine. After dinner, he would pour himself a 12-year-old Johnny Walker and light a cigar. A real professional. In the afternoon, he would set up his chair in front of the tent and admire the Goddess, lighting a cigar and smoking under her very nose.

Otherwise, at Base Camp, the circus was in full swing. Kristiano, one of the two the Poles, was copying his own notes out of books written by two of his female compatriots who had climbed Everest from Nepal; one a year ago and the other six years ago. He copied out all their notes about the peak and the environs from their books and published it all on his own page. The information he sent his sponsors was also from the books, along with his own photos. I don't think he had any idea where he was, or why he was here. At least he had read a little before he came. There were elementary things he didn't know, which I was initially very surprised at. He hadn't even heard of the monsoons. David, another Oscar deserving actor, made live broadcasts on Hungarian television and radio every day. He showed himself off dressed in old Tibetan folk costumes like a clown just sitting there without talking. His television appearances clearly earned him good money for expeditions. I thought it was ridiculous, but it's all experience. I was still learning my trade.

Everest stood there day after day, watching us waste our time instead of doing something useful. I also thought about the country house I had inherited, and wondered if it had already fallen into rack and ruin. I thought that with the money and time I had spent on this expedition, I could have rebuilt it and landscaped the ground around it. Or spent the last couple of months doing some other useful work. Time seemed to fly by so quickly here. 20 days passed in the blink of an eye. One-third of the time had passed, two-thirds remained. Another third would be spent in altitude acclimatization

The last third of the time was for climbing to the top and returning to Bulgaria. In my mind I had already climbed the peak really quickly. I'm always in a hurry and I never seem to have enough time. The top seemed so close but so inaccessible from Base Camp. Almost every morning was cloudless and the visibility perfect. What made me happiest and filled my heart was waking up every morning to see Chomolungma. It was always the first thing that appeared before my eyes when I opened the flap of my tent. There's no other sight to compare with it! The mountain filled me with energy the moment I woke up.

I got bored from time to time. I regretted not taking a book to read. I didn't even have a notebook or diary to note down my impressions. My luggage was limited and I had already exceeded the weight many times over. The limit of 30 kg for luggage is nowhere enough for anyone planning to climb Everest. I would have had to pay at least another

$300 for another 30kg... but I didn't actually have anything else I needed. There was so much equipment I didn't have. On the other hand, my emotions were so heightened I was sure I wouldn't forget anything and there was no need to note my impressions down.

Today I decided to wash all the clothes I had worn, to have clean clothes to the end.

I occasionally wondered why I was here. Wasting so much time and money, and so much misery. It didn't make much sense. And for what? I kept telling myself I had a specific goal that I wanted to prove something to myself and the world. But on the other hand, it was a foolish endeavour. Anyone who didn't believe in what I was doing would still not believe. What did I need to prove anyway? Everyone makes their own mind up about to live their lives, about what to do with it, what to eat, what to drink, who to be with and when to part.

I kept thinking about our material world and why it's structured in the way it is. Why aren't people better, more humane? When don't we help each other? The only place I had seen decent, honest people was in Germany, where I spent more than seven years. It's an exemplary country in every respect. I am just an ordinary little person. Nothing depends on me and there's nothing I can do to change anything. Yes, lots of things irritate me, especially injustice in all its shapes and sizes. However, when the Force sent me the idea that we can live to the full without killing and eating animals, it gave me great hope that I too could do something good for humanity. Perhaps I could show that anything is possible and if you have a dream, you can achieve it. I've always helped others, and I wanted to help now.

We need to stop eating animals, and live in harmony with nature and in balance with ourselves and the environment. We need to think positively, to dream and make our dreams come true. Because animals are part of us. We inhabit the same ecosystem and habitat. They too are born, think, feel, multiply and die. Why eat them when they are not our natural food and we feel better when we consume plant food? Why do we have to wait until we get seriously ill and the good doctor tells us, "The way to feel better is to stop eating meat and meat-based foods, as well as dairy products?" People still eat other people in Papua New Guinea, because it's what they're used to. There was once cannibalism in our latitudes, but now we are ashamed of it. I believe that the time will come when humanity will be ashamed that it once ate meat, just as we're ashamed that distant ancestors once ate each other.

There was a strong westerly wind blowing at the peak.

I won't go into too much detail about the digestive system of man and herbivores. There are already plenty of books, the Internet and seminars, and anyone who needs proof that we were created to eat plant foods will find plenty. However, it's a psychological process. Only one who believes will understand. I am convinced that in the future people will not eat meat for a number of reasons. One of them is that animal husbandry itself pollutes the environment. it requires huge amounts of drinking water and as I wrote at the beginning of the book, the land on which we produce animal feed is actually needed for our food - to enable the population of the planet to grow.

But let's return to Base Camp. The date is April 24, 2014.

I was thinking about what to do with my heavy sleeping bag and down-filled clothes. I had to take the sleeping bag with me to the Intermediate Camp, but I also needed the down-filled clothes for the Advance Camp. That meant that I would have to take 20 kg of luggage with me tomorrow. The last time I had an annoying suspicion that the head of the Advance Camp had slept in my bag. I had left it with him in storage for one night. Doiter's sleeping bag weighed 2,2 kg, as much as my Bulgarian one, but it was so much warmer. It was German after all.

That evening I called home to my family in Bulgaria because I was missing them very much. In Bulgaria it was warm and green. The birds were singing, the grass was growing and here there was nothing but dust, cold, stones, snow and ice. I wondered how I could reduce the weight of my luggage for tomorrow.

Everything at dinner was fine, the gas burner warmed the tent, and I felt good. The food was the same. Yesterday I had persuaded the Serdar to arrange for yaks to carry some of my luggage for $5 per kilogram to the Intermediate Camp. I didn't want to carry more than 20 kilograms over 20 kilometres. If I left the sleeping bag there, I could carry the rest to the Advance Camp myself.

DAY 20

25 April 2014

I had no intention of getting up early. There was one thing clear today, I had to get to the Intermediate Camp. At breakfast, I spoke to David and Adina, and they said that they were also leaving for the Intermediate Camp. They left immediately after breakfast. I wasn't in a hurry because some of my luggage was being taken by yak. However, when I went to see the Serdar, I realised that he had pulled the wool over my eyes. He hadn't spoken to anyone. The transport was still the next day. I was very angry, packed my bags and didn't even take any food for lunch because it was just eggs and bread. I was furious that I still had to carry my heavy rucksack along a road where yak transport was available. If only I had a thinner down-filled jacket to keep at Base Camp, I wouldn't have to carry the heavy one around all the camps ... But I didn't have the money.

I left about an hour after David and Adina and cursed all along the way. My rucksack weighed about 22 kilograms. Why were the locals so irresponsible and deceitful? From the very beginning, they lied to me about so many things and continued to lie. I still had no idea how many more problems they would create for me with their lying, irresponsibility and carelessness.

I walked relatively slowly all alone on the familiar route. I stopped occasionally to drink tea or take a bite to eat. At one point I met the Russians coming down from the Intermediate Camp. They had spent the night there and were coming back down. The Poles, the Indians, and Bill would ascend to Advance Base Camp today. I took a photo with Victor and we had a chat.

I walked and gritted my teeth. At one point I called Dava, the manager of the company in Kathmandu, to tell him that the locals here were getting out of hand, and had lied to me about the yak transport. Our Sherpas were the only ones here without a manager and they did what they wanted. I likened our camp to a dilapidated garden and the Base Camp to the "central casino". The Sherpas from all the camps came to our to gamble. It was forbidden in the other camps. From morning till night, it never stopped. On top of it all, there were the Tibetans who fixed the ropes and were all involved in their own scams. The Russian and Swiss business owners were constantly by the sides of their expeditions and helped their customers in every way possible.

A chance meeting with Victor Bobok on the way to the Intermediate Camp

After a while I caught up with David and Adina who were walking at snail's pace, I guess because of Adina. I was walking slowly too, because there was no need to hurry. I arrived at the Intermediate Camp at 5,800 metres at about 14.30. I thought that the Hungarians must have gone back down, because I hadn't seen them behind me.

The only person at the Intermediate Camp was Sambo, the manager, who didn't speak a word of English or any other language. So there was no communication. I explained to him that I wanted to have dinner at 6 pm and that I wanted him to cook me something. The previous week I had slept in a single tent in the highest part of camp, but this time I took a double tent at the bottom. I wanted to have a bit more room.

It was a nice sunny day and it was 20 degrees inside. I took advantage of the warmth and took a "shower" with wet wipes. They were very refreshing. I was still angry that I had had to carry my heavy rucksack along a road where there were plenty of yaks. My feet were in a really bad state because of that rucksack. Just my luck no yaks were going to make the ascent further up, so there was no one to ask to take my rucksack for me. As soon as I approached Intermediate Camp, they began to overtake me ... but there wasn't any point. It had been a difficult day for me. Getting to the roof of the world is no easy matter. I vowed never to walk with a heavy rucksack again. I could barely use my legs. This wasn't tourism, but masochism and all pleasure of mountaineering had vanished without a trace.

I lay down and thought to myself that here I am spending the night higher than the highest peak in Europe - Mount Elbrus, 5642 metres. The sun was still shining, and it was warm, at least for here. The sound of large stones and boulders tumbling from the neighbouring slopes could be heard loudly. It was 6.30 pm and I was getting quite hungry. So I went to the cook to see what he was doing. The Hungarians also appeared. They had made it. The cook poured us a cup of tea first. Then he made vegetable soup from a packet, adding fresh onions. The main meal was boiled rice with dal. He made omelettes for the Hungarians. I filmed the whole preparation of the dinner with the camera. I hope to make a film about my ascent of Chomolungma. It was a lot of fun watching the food being prepared. There was absolutely no hygiene and the only thing that saved us from an epidemic was that we were at 5800 metres. David asked me not film him because he was a big star and didn't want anyone to post pictures of him. He reckoned he was a big cheese, the poor deluded man. Then again, it's no easy feat coming here for a seventh time.

Dinner was delicious and plentiful. It didn't really matter anymore that there was no protein in the food ... Horses don't eat protein and they can run and carry heavy things. Or bulls, they only eats grass, yet they're so strong.

I went to bed right after dinner, it was still light outside.

Day 21

April 26 2014

The night was calm and warm, the temperatures barely dropped to minus 8 degrees in the tent. The morning sun was warm and I warmed up quickly. There were pancakes with jam for breakfast. Adina returned to Base Camp, and David headed for Advance Base Camp an hour before me. I was in no hurry, and after breakfast I rested in the tent. I didn't feel like leaving, knowing how far I had to walk with this rucksack. In an effort to reduce my luggage, I left my 2.2 kilogram sleeping bag in the Intermediate Camp, as well as some clothes and ate the food I had left over from yesterday. My backpack was about three or four kilograms lighter, but it was still quite heavy.

All the groups from the other companies passed my tent in the direction of the Advance Base Camp. At one point, I decided to get a move on as well. The sun was hot, but the wind was blowing and it was cold. Try as I might, I couldn't walk slowly, and little by little I started to catch up with the others in front of me and overtake them. On my first break I caught up with the Russians, about 16 of them. I chatted to a couple of them. Completely ordinary people out on an excursion.

However, they had the best equipment, guides and huge quantities of oxygen bottles. They were trying very hard. In the second resting spot, I caught up with David who was about to leave, but I decided to stop for a rest anyway. There was no point in exhausting myself and rushing ahead. The second rest was in a tent by some lakes. The view was so breathtaking. I ate what I was carrying and carried on upwards. Heavy as it was, it had to be carried. No one had made me come here, so I shouldn't complain. I had wished it upon myself and I really wanted to be here. After this resting spot in the tent, the scenery became incredibly beautiful.

The Russian expedition between the Intermediate and Advance Camp

This time it was a little different because the weather was a little warmer and the rivers were flowing. Other ice formations had receded. I was fascinated by how much the scenery had changed in the space of just a week. I overtook David just before Advance Camp. There were lots of yaks going in both directions on the way. About midway, I met the two Indians and Bill returning to Base Camp after a night at Advance Camp. There were just Poles left in the camp. I arrived shortly after 1 pm and the others were having lunch.

The chef made canned beans, cabbage salad and a pancake. He heated up the beans with onions and spices and it was delicious. But there only two cans of beans. I had a hearty meal and drank two cups of tea. I was planning to stay a week at Advance Camp and sleep for one night at Camp 1 North Col. However, I still didn't know that altitude is something to be taken seriously, no matter what plans you might make. After lunch, I spent some time alone in my tent. I felt very tired... after all it was 6440 metres above sea level ... And that rucksack.

I lay in the tent and wondered, "What are all these people doing here, so high up?" At 1500-2000 metres above sea level, everything is so beautiful, green, and warm, ... here there's nothing but rocks, scree, snow and ice. Then I asked myself, "What am I doing here?" There wasn't just one answer. I wanted to see the limits of a vegan. Do vegans have limits? Maybe not. I was there to explore the Power of the Spirit and offer my knowledge and experience to other people, so that they can make their dreams come true, especially when it comes to reducing the amount of animal food we eat.

I waited for the tent to warm up a bit and took out the wet wipes to take a shower. The wipes froze every night and thawed during the day. This happened with all the liquids and chocolates I was carrying. Today I brought more medicines with me from Base Camp to the Advance Base Camp. This would be my base camp now.

In the afternoon I took a walk around. I was astonished at how many camps and tents there were. In terms of its area, it was much smaller than Base camp, but there needed to be room for everyone.

The two Poles, David and I had dinner together. The Poles planned to go up to Camp 1 the next day and return to sleep here, and I planned to go to the wall at 6,650 metres and return here for a second night. Everyone had their own programme and goal.

After dinner I went outside to look at the sky and the stars. I shot some video of the illuminated tents of the Chinese Mountain Service. They had electricity in every tent and they shone like a beacon every night. Nowhere on earth is there such beauty. It was like a tale of fairies and elves. So beautiful and mysterious.

Day 22

April 27 2014

I slept for the second time in my life at 6440 metres. The first time was last week. I slept well. It wasn't too cold and actually quite bearable. There was a strong wind in the morning, and although it was sunny, it felt colder. After breakfast I decided to take an acclimatization walk to the base of the wall, where the fixed guide rope begins at an altitude of about 6650 metres. My plan for the next day was to ascend to Camp 1 at 7100 metres and then go back down to sleep at the Advance Base Camp. Then I would rest for a day and go back to Camp 1 and spend the night. I made this acclimatization program myself. That day, Kristiano and Richard set out before me with the intention to ascend and then go back down to sleep at 6,440 metres. I walked to the base of the wall by myself. The path was clearly marked. Our camp was almost at the top, only the Russians were above us. The comfortable and luxurious Russian tents here too were larger than ours.

Crampon Spot before the North Col wall

Between Intermediate and Advance Base camp

At first you walk over rocks and stones, then gradually a little ice and snow begin to appear. You reach an elevation where antennas and transmitters are mounted. The path carries on descending slightly and follows the path of a frozen river. After about an hour of very slow walking, I reached the crampon spot. There are several plastic barrels, and each company has its own one where members can leave their seats, crampons and ice- picks. Our company had not yet installed its barrel yet, but it was still too early. I had my crampons in my rucksack and left them here.

I hadn't used them since Lenin Peak last year. Four months earlier, on my first climb to 6,600 metres in Aconcagua, I realised that I could do it without crampons and the second time I didn't even bother taking them with me. That's how I climbed it - without crampons.

I had new boots which I had bought especially for Everest, just for this section from 6400 metres to 7300 metres. I didn't want to use my heavy and triple-layered boots which are designed for the peak, not for acclimatization. If I'd bought them earlier, before Aconcagua, they would been ideal. From 4400 metres upwards I always used my high-altitude boots which are not intended for clambering over stones and rocks. Their soles wear off very quickly. I didn't need such warm boots either. I got the job done. Now I had the boots I didn't have before. With my crampons on my boots, I turned left and ascended towards some flags placed as a landmark. I was walking on the ice of the Rong Pu glacier itself. It starts here and almost reaches Base Camp. There is a large, wide section that has to be crossed diagonally before you reach the base of the wall. I could see people climbing the wall. The Poles were there too, about to go up. I was in no hurry and enjoyed the beautiful day and the views.

It was easy to walk on the ice with crampons, but on several occasions, my leg fell through the ice surface right up to my knee. This was both dangerous and unpleasant. There were also small fissures I needed to jump over, and I sincerely hoped that larger ones wouldn't open up.

In front of me rose the entire wall in all its majesty. It was awe-inspiring, so many people had died here. A wondrous and beautiful wall, covered in ice, snow, crevasses, caves, gutters, canopies, dangerous overhangs and everything else you can think of in the snow-covered winter mountains. About 20 minutes later, I reached the place where climbers left their sticks and ten metres further on the guide ropes started. The Poles hadn't made much progress. I could see them about 50 metres away from me. I stayed at the base of the wall for a while, studying it carefully. I decided that the day was right for me to go to Camp 1 as well. I had slept at 6440 metres last week, and I reckoned there wouldn't be any problem with climbing it today. However, I didn't have my harness, Jumara of any other such equipment. I realised it was a mistake that I hadn't gone to Camp 1 today.

This wall was nothing like the wall at Mount Lenin, which I climbed twice last year. This wall was high, steep, and irresistible. I carefully studied the challenge for tomorrow and bade my farewells.

North Col wall, from 6650 to 7100 metres, North Face, Everest

The return journey is always much faster. I retraced my steps through the large meadow of ice and snow to the place where climbers removed their crampons. From there it took 40 minutes back to camp for lunch. Chef Nuri had become my friend and he made me something delicious. I had brought a packet of powdered Chlorella with me, but I never opened it because I had frequent diarrhoea. Chlorella and spirulina have an additional laxative effect. I also had some out of date vegan bars, but I didn't dare to eat them either. So I gave them to my Sherpa and the others. I also had some bio-chocolates with me which froze so hard at night that they could only be eaten in the afternoon. I brought half of them back with me to Bulgaria. At that altitude, I felt a little tired. After lunch, I took my customary "shower" with wet wipes and rested in the tent. I was thinking about my acclimatization tactics. However, the only thing you have to listen to here are your body and your head. Programmes and schemes play little part.

The Poles returned from Camp 1 for dinner. Kristiano looked very tired and exhausted. The next day they planned to descend to Base Camp. I arranged with my Sherpa Gilgen to come with me to Camp 1. We agreed to start after breakfast. Nothing out of the ordinary happened in the evening. After dinner, when I was alone in the tent, I thought about my loved ones. Most about all I missed my son. I tried to call them every 2-3 days on the satellite phone, but I kept the conversations to a minimum because it is an expensive pleasure.

DAY 23

28 April 2014

THE DAY OF TRUTH. I couldn't wait to get up and go to Camp 1. This would be the highest altitude I had climbed to since the day I was born - 7100 metres. That wasn't the thing that excited me; it was actually the climb up the wall itself.

I hadn't climbed with a Jumara so far, except a couple of days before the expedition in some scree near Sliven, and then only for an hour. After breakfast, Gilgen and I packed our bags and began briskly walking along the path I had taken yesterday to the base of the wall. We walked quickly, and pretty soon we reached the place where all the barrels were. We deposited out harnesses, carabineers, Jumaras, crampons and started over the glacier. At the base of the wall I put my helmet on, not so much to protect me from anything, but because I had a camera attached to it to take pictures with. Most of the pictures I took were with the camera provided to me by Drift. I didn't need the helmet here. There was no risk of rock or ice fall. And if something did happen, the entire mountain would come down on top of you, God forbid, and there would be no chance of survival.

I put one of my sticks down at the base of the wall and put on my helmet. I attached the Jumara to the rope and went on in front. I gave the Drift to Gilgen who was behind me to take pictures, and to help if anything untoward happened. It was a steep climb to begin with. Not so bad, but it requires agility and training. Every 30-40 metres there were wedges driven into the rock face. The Jumara and safety carabineer has to be passed over the guide rope. I quickly grasped this exercise.

I hadn't been out with Gilgen before, but I quickly found out he was a rugged man. We picked up a fast pace and overtook everyone in front of us. I was having a lot of fun. We jumped over fissures, and only metres away from us there were precipices and caves big enough for a train to enter. There was as much adrenaline as you could wish for. Such incredible beauty. We caught up with a group of Chinese men who were barely crawling. About midway we caught up with David and his Sherpa and walked with them for quite a while. Then we overtook them too. In several places the wall was almost vertical. The going get quite tough here, and I really needed to pump the Jumara ascender grip quite hard. We rested in three places, drank tea and ate sweets. At the top we met a few Sherpas from our camp who had already been up before us today to leave tents, food, oxygen and other things for the expedition.

Gilgen told me that he hadn't believed I would make it up so quickly. The higher we climbed, the more amazing the view became, and the greater the danger. I especially liked this combination. Midway there were some aluminium ladders you climb up and then continue up using the rope. Each year the guide rope is a different colour. This year it was red. There were guide ropes in different colours left over from previous years. Here on the wall, the route was different each year, depending on the avalanches. Broken ropes (guide ropes) could be seen to the left and right, 20-30 metres or so from us.

It was a great experience and physical workout. You have to pull with your hands and squeeze with your legs. It took us an hour and a half to climb from the base of the wall to the camp. Very fast for a first time.

Camp 1 North Col at 7100 metres below Chomolungma peak and the northern edge

The Chinese had set up camp, but the other companies were still pitching their tents. Gilgen told me that our camp would be just below the Chinese one. I didn't like the place. There was an overhang just above us ... but there wasn't much room on the saddle. We stayed there for about half an hour to rest, drank some tea, ate something sweet, and took some pictures.

Today I had reached 7100 metres and I was very happy, not because of the altitude we had reached, but the beauty of the view. Everest looked so close. The entire route to the top can be seen so wonderfully from Camp 1. Only 1600 metres ascent to the top. If we hadn't been at such an altitude, it would have been precisely a day's work to get to the top and back, if not just a couple of hours. Perhaps just one day.

A little later, David and his Sherpa arrived. They would be spending the night in Camp 1 tonight and going back down to the Advance Base Camp tomorrow. I don't know why I decided to go to Camp 1 without spending the night there, and then ascend again to spend the night a day or two later. I still don't know why idea occurred to me, but it was a big mistake. I should have spent my first night in Camp 1 yesterday or today and then go down to rest in Base Camp.

I felt good at 7,100 metres in Camp 1, and I was already regretting that we hadn't brought our sleeping bags to sleep here. We would see if we could make the climb again the next day.

We headed on back down the steep path. Although the descent was rapid, it took a lot of strength and concentration. Every single step has to be precise and very well judged. We didn't rappel down. We just attached our carabineers to the guide rope and held the rope. If you lose your grip, you end up flying down to the next wedge or person. But that's how everyone descended. It took a lot of effort in some places. We descended very quickly without breaks. I still had no idea that the next couple of times I climbed and descended the wall, I wouldn't be so fast. We got down to the base of the wall where I retrieved my other stick. Then we headed across the glacier to the barrels to leave our seats, crampons and equipment for our next climb.

In front of Camp 1, North Col, 7,100 metres

In the tent at Advance Base Camp, 6440 metres

About half an hour later we were drinking tea in the Advance Base

Camp at 6440 metres. I had been carrying the thick down jacket with me all day and it was weighing me down a lot. However, I didn't know what the weather would be like in Camp 1 or on the way. The forecast was for perfect weather, but here everything changes so quickly.

To be honest, it's no easy task to climb the wall, especially with luggage on your back. Nor is the descent an easy matter either. My plan was to rest in the Advance Camp the next day, and then after five nights at 6440 metres, ascend to sleep at a greater altitude. I was definitely tired and intended to relax the next day. Today I was the only member in the Advance Base Camp. Everyone else had gone back down, and David had stayed in Camp 1 to sleep there. I felt happy. I called my relatives to tell them that everything was fine.

DAY 24

April 29 2014

Third consecutive night at 6440 metres and fourth for the expedition. It snowed during the night, and in the morning there was about two or three inches, nothing to worry about. When the sun came up, it melted. I didn't sleep very well at night, and I was a little bloated in the morning. My plan was to rest today and go to Camp 1 tomorrow to spend the night there. However, I didn't feel very well. I decided to see how I would feel during the day and then make a decision. Was it too early for me to sleep at 7,100 metres, or should I have stayed there last night?

It was David's seventh time here and he had spent countless nights over 7,000 metres. He had reached 8,500 metres two or three times, and had also climbed Shisha-pangma and Cho Oyu before embarking on Everest ten years ago. I wasn't comparing myself to him and I wasn't very interested in his tactics. I didn't think he was a very sensible man with his demonstrative lifestyle of eating, drinking, and smoking, as well his attitude, manners and so much more. He had also been my tent partner at the Advance Base Camp, where he had arrived with so much luggage.

At least of 100 kilograms of which was just his food and dozens of cans of drink. He also had a big solar panel and a huge device for storing the energy. Out of curiosity, I picked it up to see how heavy the battery was, it was some weight. I even took a photograph of it. He had no end of cans, bags and boxes all covered his sponsors' stickers. At least I saw how an expedition should be organised. Hopefully one day I will be lucky enough to take everything I need for an expedition. Ready-made juices, soft drinks in cans and alcohol, well I don't drink alcohol and I don't need them, but if I had a solar kit and a laptop...

I spent all day by myself in the camp and rested for most of the time. The gamblers only broke off for lunch. I walked around the camp, but I wasn't feeling 100 percent. I started wondering whether it was a good idea to sleep in Camp 1 tomorrow or and go back down to Base Camp. The others spent a maximum of two or three nights at 6,400 metres and then went back down. Tonight would be my fourth in a row and fifth since the beginning of the expedition. I have never put so much stress on my body at such an altitude, but there's always a first time.

My tent at the Advance Base Camp, 6440 metres, and the place where the Puja ritual took place.

I didn't have anything to read here either, and it was very cold too. It was sunny, but still cold in the tents. I packed myself up in my sleeping bag and began to meditate. In the afternoon the two Russians turned up. Victor definitely had experience at altitude, and I asked him for advice about my situation. He was adamant that I should go down immediately. It was a marvellous achievement that I had made it to 7100 metres yesterday, but I needed to go down right away today, especially since I had already spent four nights in a row at 6440 metres. He recommended I go down tomorrow. There was no point in rushing so much with acclimatization. I'd done a good job by getting to Camp 1.

I still wanted to try for an oxygen-free climb, and my plan even included spending a night in Camp 2 at 7,700 metres before the hike to the top. Victor and I talked a lot, and there was logic in his words. His personal opinion was that it was pointless and utter madness to climb Everest without oxygen. His plan was to take his client to sleep that night at 6,440 metres for the first time, just for one night, and then go back down to Base Camp. The next time they would climb to 7100 metres without sleeping in Camp 1, and thus complete their acclimatization. Then as they trekked to the summit, they would put on their oxygen masks at 7100 metres. He had done this three times before and it worked well. As a rule, the use of oxygen reduces the displacement level by about 2000 metres. The level in the oxygen bottle levels is, of course, very important. There's always the risk of damaging something on the mask, bottle or regulator.

David returned that evening with his Sherpa. He looked very bad. He had no strength left and could barely stand on his feet. Sleeping at 7,100 metres and then climbing to 7,500 metres during the day had been too much for him to bear. So there were four of us now in the Advance Camp.

It was very cold at dinner time, there was a problem with the gas burner, and we couldn't keep warm. I didn't know what to do. Should I go to Camp 1 again in the morning or return to Base Camp. I decided to sleep on it and take the decision in the morning. During the night there was a strong wind and it began snowing.

David's tent, his solar park and the energy storage battery

Day 25

30 April 2014

The winds whistled all night long, and it was very cold. I couldn't sleep, my heart was racing and I didn't need any heart monitor to tell me. My heart was pounding as if I was running a marathon. I decided to check my heart rate accurately in the morning. Using my watch I measured out a minute, and with my fingers on the carotid artery, I counted the beats. The first time it was 133, and the second - 130 beats per minute. I needed to descend immediately.

I could have slept at 7,100 metres the other day and then gone back down to Base Camp, but I already slept for four consecutive nights at 6,440 metres. To stay any longer would be detrimental to my health. I hadn't felt well since yesterday. I decided to go down. I had no appetite for breakfast. I would not be at the Advance Base Camp on the 2nd of

May, so I left my Drift camera with Gilgen to film the Puja ritual, as well as some money for the Lama to mention me in his prayers. I explained to him how to take pictures, grabbed my luggage and went down as quickly as I could. On the way I met the two Russians. Victor was walking quickly, but Alex was in no hurry. The oligarch had completed the Iron Man course two years ago and was in good shape, but the altitude was bothering him. I decided to walk with them and talk. Alex didn't like talking and was quite conceited. However, Victor was talkative and companionable. Actually Victor is Ukrainian, he just lives in Russia. He told me plenty of interesting stories about his expeditions over the past 35 years. I was especially interested in his 2004 expedition to Everest because the Bulgarian national mountaineering team had taken part, exactly where we were now.

Alex and me before Advance Base Camp at about 6,200 metres.

His memories were still fresh and he told me some interesting facts. First he told me that he admired Hristo Prodanov and the 1984 expedition to the Western Ridge. He had also read a book about the expedition and was very impressed. He also knew the old Bulgarian climbers by the names in his book, and they had been an example to him. However, he said with a sneer that he couldn't understand why the best Bulgarian climbers in 2004 decided to take the amateur tourist route, rather than the North Wall or at least something that needed to be climbed. Then he shared his personal opinion that after Prodanov's death there was no real mountaineering in Bulgaria. I said nothing. I have no idea why they chose this route ten years ago, or who took part. The only member of that expedition I knew was Ivan Temelkov, but I didn't know any of the details. Victor also told me about Mariana and about her participation in a Russian expedition in 2004. He knew her well and had often talked to her about the expedition. He told me how on June 1, 2004, after reaching the top of the north wall, and on his way down the North Edge, he found her a little below the top, took some pictures of her and then sent them back to Bulgaria. I felt very sad for a person I didn't even know. He felt very sad for Mariana as well and always thought of her whenever he saw me. He was sure that she had reached the top because she was only 40-50 metres below him and had died on the way back when she stopped to rest. He described the place to me so that I could look around for her if I got there in a few days.

Victor also told me about his expeditions to Antarctica, and how in the space of two weeks he had skied from the South Pole to the ocean. He told me about his expeditions to Carstenz, Denali and other peaks. It was fascinating and I enjoyed listening to him. I also wanted to go to Antarctica, Carstenz and Denali soon, but they were still a dream.

About three hours later we reached the Intermediate Camp, where my sleeping bag was waiting in storage. We had some spaghetti, rested, and continued down to Base Camp. Alex could barely walk and was already beginning to stumble. We walked slowly for him and took frequent breaks. There were a lot of yaks all the way. It was the fourth time I had walked this route. Just before Intermediate Camp we met the Indians, the Poles, and Bill, who were planning to spend the night there. The next day they were going to go to the Advance Base so that they could take part in the Puja ritual on the morning of May 2nd. I wanted to go too, but because of my acclimatization I wouldn't be there. Victor told me that the next day he and Alex were going back down to Zangmu at 2,300 metres to rest. I really liked the idea and decided to go with them to save on the cost of transport by jeep. In the late afternoon we arrived at Base Camp. As always I was loaded like an infantryman. We left our luggage and Victor and I went to the camp officer to arrange transport.

He was about a kilometre away. We found him and told him what we wanted. He told us that the jeep from Base Camp to Zangmu would cost $920 one way. I almost fainted… it was only about 230 kilometres. Of course, we would need it in both directions which meant $ 1,840. Daylight robbery. Then we asked him for a price to Tingri which is 90 kilometres away. It was a tolerable $200 each way. So we agreed that at 10 o'clock the next day a jeep would come to pick up all three of us.

The rocks above the Tibetan camp, 5500 metres

Rest between the Intermediate and Base Camp, about 5550 metres

DAY 26

May 1 2014

That night after four nights at 6440 metres, I slept like a baby. I didn't wake up to drink water or go to the toilet. I don't know how many hours I slept, but I woke up only when the sun had warmed the tent so much that I could barely breathe inside. Oxygen is such a big deal. Yesterday, as I was going down, I began to breathe more calmly with each step I took and my pulse dropped. I had no intention of going to Tingri, but when the opportunity arose with the two Russians, I agreed. The Russians didn't have any cash, so I agreed to pay for the jeep, and then they would give me back half.

After breakfast as we were packing our bags, a jeep turned up with two Indians who were on an American expedition. They weren't feeling well after spending the night at 6,400 metres and were giving up. They were going back to England where they lived. The officer said we could join them for $100, so we all got in with the Indians, and he didn't call for a second jeep. We agreed. It was a little cramped for the four on the back seat, but it was better than waiting for another jeep, and it would only cost us $33 each to get to Tingri.

It was good thing the Russians and I had almost no luggage. The two Indians had filled the boot of the Land Cruiser to the seams. The driver was a Tibetan. On the way we talked to the Indians and they told us that they were travelling to Zangmu. They would spend the night there, and the next day they would travel to Nepal. That was the route we would all take. We asked how much it would cost for us to travel with them to Zangmu, but they were greedy and sly and asked us for another $300 per person. I didn't have that sort of money, and I flatly refused. The Russians had no cash. It was thanks to me they were able to get down to Tingri at all. It wasn't the most comfortable journey - four men crammed into the back seat, but we survived for three hours. It was a good job that all four of us were thin.

We arrived for lunch in Tingri at the same hotel where we slept for two nights on arrival. This time we had to pay for everything ourselves, and the prices were pretty high. The hotel was $50 per bed per night, and the price for three meals was $ 25, or $75 per day, plus the transportation to get there. We had a good lunch in the restaurant at the hotel, I was happy because they had prepared tofu, mushrooms, lettuce, and rice, especially for me. I ate very well. The Russians, however, especially Alex, didn't want to stay in Tingri, but to go down to Zangmu, where there was everything a city could offer. It turned out that there was no ATM in Tingri and money could only be withdrawn in Zangmu.

Victor found transport for the next day to take them to Zangmu where they would spend one night and return on the third of May. I think they agreed to about $800 in both directions. I really wanted to go down to Zangmu too, because I already knew from my trip to Aconcagua how important it was to descend to a lower altitude to rest and recharge your blood and especially your brain with oxygen. However, the multimillionaire was tight-fisted and didn't want me to go with them unless we split the costs. If it hadn't been for me, they would still be in Base Camp. That's what most rich people are like - egotistical and selfish. All Alex wanted to do was smoke marijuana and suggested that I try some too. I've never smoked a cigarette in my life, I don't even know what coffee tastes like, and here he was offering me grass... ... His attitude really upset me. If I had the same financial might as him, I would have taken everyone in the jeep at my own expense. He was going to pay for the whole jeep anyway, and the price would be the same whether there were two or three passengers. That's clearly what oligarchs are like. It would best suit him if I could pay for everything.

After the meal, I went for a short walk outside and took some pictures with the camera. Nothing around surprised me, I had been here already two weeks ago. The same dogs, cows and yaks competing for waste from restaurants and houses. A pathetic picture.

I went back to my room and bathed. The best bath of my life. The last time I had bathed was on April 9 in Kathmandu, and the last time I had washed my hair was in Sliven, on April 5. This was my new record for the longest period without bathing and washing my hair - 26 days. Not that my hair was so dirty... after the tenth day it was still quite oily, but a lot of it had fallen out because of the altitude. I'd already had a similar experience on Lenin Peak where it fell out in handfuls, but after I returned to Bulgaria it recovered in a few weeks. So I wasn't too concerned.

It was so nice to take a hot shower after more than 20 days of freezing cold and misery. I couldn't have enjoyed the hot water more. I also hadn't shaved in a month, ever since the last time in Sliven. I decided to experiment with different styles for my beard. It wasn't easy spending 20 days at altitude. It's a good job I didn't have any scissors so I couldn't experiment with hairstyles as well. It was another personal record - bathing at 4400 metres above sea level. I'll never forget it. I enjoyed the hot water in the shower so much. I must have left half of my hair in the bathroom. I was a bit worried that the maid might think that I had cut my hair in the shower, but it was just falling out. Now I really appreciated how nice it is to take a bath and wash your locks. Then lie down in clean, white sheets, it was ultra, mega, hyper luxury. That's why the Chinese charged an arm and a leg, because they knew how important it was for the climbers to be bathed and clean.

The temperature in the room was 16 degrees, and I felt hot. Usually I feel cold at about 20 degrees, and now it was only 16 and I felt hot. Altitude has such an effect on the body! In addition to acclimatizing, I had obviously become inured to the cold as well. My hair was no joke, and I was pleased to find a hair dryer in the room to dry it a little. I went to bed, pleased that I hadn't continued to Camp 1 yesterday, but had gone back down to Base Camp and now I was lying in white sheets. I felt brand new and ready for new achievements. When I thought about it, it wasn't so bad in the tent either. I had become so used to this tent that it felt like my home.

Tomorrow I would spend all the day resting in Tingri to recuperate, and on the 3rd of May I would wait for the Russians to pick me up and take me to Base Camp. I would go back up to the higher altitudes to continue my acclimatization. My goal was to sleep in Camp 1 at 7100 metres and the next day climb as high as possible. I had already decided that I would use oxygen, especially after my conversation with Victor, and taking my physical condition into consideration as well. I was quite exhausted, I had been eating nothing but rice, potatoes and spaghetti for a long time. David didn't look at all well after sleeping at 7100 metres. I decided to wait and see. I still had time to acclimatize, but things were already leaning toward oxygen.

I slept so soundly and well last night at Base Camp just because there was more oxygen in the air. Oxygen is a pretty big deal. Did I really need to climb get oxygen-free and punish my body so harshly? It's perfectly possible to climb oxygen-free ascent. Reinhold Messner and Peter Habeler did it in 1978. Over the past 36 years, more than 280 people have climbed Everest without oxygen. I wouldn't be proving anything new. On the other hand, no vegan had set foot on the Roof of the World and that was the challenge for me.

At dinner, I made friends with one of the cooks who knew a few words of English, and she made me a very tasty dinner. Then I went upstairs to my room to see what it was like sleeping at 4,400 metres.

DAY 27

May 2 2014

How nice it is to sleep in a bed with white and clean sheets. The best part of it all is that I don't have to walk 200 metres to the toilet or pee in a bottle at night.

We had doughnuts, spaghetti with vegetables and some mushrooms for breakfast. It was a strange breakfast, but it was very tasty. I had lost a lot of weight and welcomed any sort of food. Then I went for a walk and bought some fruit. The animals on the road were still fighting over the household slops. There are only a handful of wells with water here, and people carry it in vessels tied to their backs. The well which was in the yard of our hotel was used by the same people who come for water dozens of times every day. One young girl was always coming and carried 25 litres of water on her back.

A girl carrying water from a well, Tingri.

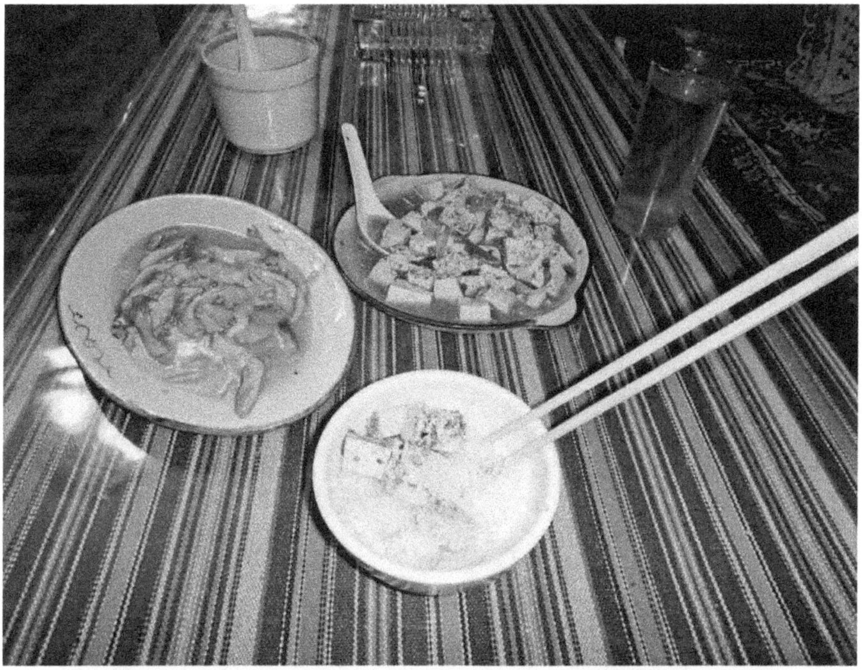

My dinner - tofu with spices, mushrooms, rice and green tea

After the bath

I washed everything I had with me by hand in the bathroom and hung it all over the room to dry. The sun was shining and the room was quite warm. I hoped the laundry would dry by tomorrow, and the Russians wouldn't be here until 1 p.m. At lunch, I also ate a lot of Tibetan specialties and spent the whole afternoon in the room. I turned on the television but all the channels were in Chinese and I didn't understand anything. I hadn't watched television in three years, but out of boredom I turned it on. I found a show where people with different talents were performing in front of a jury. I saw such unique Chinese people and all the manner of things they could do.

For dinner I ordered pan-fried tofu prepared with hot spices, very tasty mushrooms and rice. I ordered green tea to drink. After dinner I watched some TV again and went to bed to rest.

Day 28

May 3 2014

I spent a second night in the town of Tingri at 4400 metres. I slept well. The temperature dropped to 3-4 degrees in the room at night, but it was nice and warm under the thick quilt. My room faced southeast, and as when the sun rose after 9 o'clock, it warmed up quickly. I had the same breakfast as the day before and went out for a walk on the dusty streets of Tingri. The streets were full of all kinds of animals, and because there were no garbage cans, all the waste was discarded behind the houses.

The town was to all intents and purposes one large central street, with buildings and houses on both sides, and the fields behind these buildings and houses are used as garbage dumps. Everything behind the houses is a big dump, where dogs, yaks, cows and people all rummage together. It was so filthy. There wasn't really anywhere to take a walk. It takes half an hour to walk the entire street on both sides. There were all kinds of shops, mainly for groceries and clothes, as well as workshops and car and motorcycle repair shops. At noon I returned to the hotel to have something to eat and hoped that the Russians would come soon. It was 14 o'clock and they still hadn't arrived. I started getting worried that something might have happened. I had packed my bags and was waiting for them downstairs in the restaurant. It was 15 o'clock, and still no sign of them. Something must have happened. We forgot to exchange phone numbers, and I couldn't call them. They had gone to Zangmu yesterday before breakfast and I never saw them again.

It was not until 16.00 Chinese time (around 14.00 Nepali time) that the jeep appeared, but only Victor got out. Clearly something had happened to Alexander. Victor explained to me that Alex hadn't been feeling well and had left Zangmu for London today. Victor was returning to Base Camp to pack up their luggage. We got in the jeep and headed for Base Camp. It was the same driver as the other day. He was driving quite fast, but the car started having problems. It couldn't maintain speed and stalled on a number of occasions. We stopped several times to cool it down with snow. It would only go in first gear, second at most, and in third packed up altogether. Victor was getting quite angry, but I didn't really care. When we stopped for the third time, we decided to transfer into another car, if there was anyone to take us. It was the high season at the moment and there was a lot of traffic on the road. A minibus with three Chinese people in it immediately stopped and they took us. We were saved.

Around 18.00 we arrived at Rong Pu Monastery, and I asked if I could get out to have a look. I wanted them to offer a Puja ritual for me, since I had missed yesterday's at the Advance Base Camp. I entered the monastery, but it was empty. The hall on the first floor was locked. I climbed the steps upstairs to the hall with the large statue. A monk was beating a tradition and reciting prayers in one of the side rooms. I didn't want to interrupt him, but he noticed me. First he sold me a ticket for the monastery, then I tried to explain to him what I wanted and he called another monk on his mobile and said that they would open the hall downstairs for me. I went downstairs again, waited ten minutes, but no one came. So I went upstairs again to see the monk. He called again and this time told me that the monk was waiting for me downstairs. The hall downstairs was now open and the lama was waiting for me. I went inside and started praying. The lama was standing behind me. After a while, nuns began to enter too. I sat down next to one and she asked me my name. I explained to her that I was going to Chomolungma and needed the blessing of the Gods. They laughed. The other nuns also asked for my name and began to repeat it. One of the nuns offered me some tea.

At one point, Victor entered angrily and told me he couldn't wait for me anymore, and left. I got up and went to the lama, he took my head in both hands and rested it on his head so that the upper parts of our foreheads touched. He spoke some words that I didn't understand, but I felt that it was a prayer to the Gods - asking them to let me reach the summit and come down safe and sound. I ran out of the monastery to the waiting minibus. Where was Victor in such a hurry to? For him, the expedition was over and he had been paid $5,000. There were hundreds of yaks in front of the monastery preventing me from getting to the car quickly. I was happy with my meeting with the lama. I realised that the Chinese were in no hurry at all, and it was only the Ukrainian Victor who was so uptight.

The damaged jeep on the road between Tingri and Base Camp

Rong Pu Monastery, 5000 metres

It was still light when we arrived at Base Camp for dinner. David was the only person there, still resting. Victor explained to me that he had to go up to the Advance Base Camp and arrange for the baggage - his and his client's - to be dropped off at the Base Camp and then leave with their entire luggage. However, before that, he would try to find a new client for $ 5,000. He was happy that he his client had paid him without having to climb to the top with him. However, he hoped someone from the Russian expedition would hire him. Victor had worked for this same Russian company for 12 years and knew the owner and staff very well. The Russians were at the Advance Base Camp and there was no one in the Base Camp to ask. In principle, there was one guide for every three Russians, but he hoped someone would hire him as a personal guide. He said to me quite categorically that without a client and without being paid for it, he would never climb to the top or trek in the mountains. All the professionals saw in the mountains was a way of making money and nothing more. Why are they all alike, all over the world? It's the same in Bulgaria. It's clearly quite normal. I couldn't understand why, after he had everything he needed for the expedition — oxygen, Sherpas, food, and tents, — he didn't want to climb the summit again. I would have stayed and given it another go. Obviously we humans are very different.

My plan was to go to Intermediate Camp the next day to spend the night there, and then get to Advance Base Camp for the 5th May, and sleep at Camp 1 North Cole at 7,100 metres on the 6th May.

Mingma, the Serdar who had gone to Nepal to bury his father appeared in the camp, despite saying he wouldn't return. He had got back from Nepal yesterday and explained to me that he had done so for our sake, to ensure we got to the top. Several tents, including the Sherpa's dining tent, were full of goods waiting for the end of the expedition to be taken to Nepal with the rest of the luggage. That was the main reason he had returned to Base Camp and gamble. He was clearly good at it and fleeced the other players. But that didn't interest me.

After dinner, I lay down again in my favourite tent and got into the cigarette-smelling sleeping bag. I wanted to rip off the head of that Tibetan from Intermediate Camp who had slept in mine while it was in storage. Anyway, I was once again in the embrace of the Goddess, watching her from my tent.

Day 29

May 4, 2014

During the night I drank water for acclimatization. It was cold and windy. In the morning there was a strong wind, but the top was clearly visible. I had breakfast and said goodbye

to Victor who was in a hurry to leave without luggage and reach the Advance Base Camp in a single day without spending the night at Intermediate. I wondered if I shouldn't go directly to the Advance Camp, but I decided that there was no point in taking a risk since, at an altitude of over 5,200 metres, the body is unable to recover. Victor himself admitted that he was going straight there because he was leaving the expedition and had nothing to save his strength for.

Before I left for Intermediate Camp, one of the Sherpas found a sack in the provisions store depot and asked me if it was my food. I almost fainted - it was the food that I had bought with Dava in Kathmandu! I didn't know whether to laugh or cry, but I was furious that no one had found it for a whole month. I had been told that Chinese customs had confiscated it. Of course, things were missing. There were no beans, chickpeas, lentils or peas. But all the nuts, dried fruit, and pulses were still there. The mice had even gnawed at the dried fruit. I was very angry with these Sherpas. I didn't know if it was deliberate or they had just inadvertently found my food. Anyway, the expedition was coming to an end and I had survived without nuts for a month. In about ten minutes, I was going to the Intermediate Camp and I couldn't take more than 200-300 grams. I would be returning to Base Camp 4 days later.

I packed my bags calmly and at about 10.30 I went to the Intermediate Camp alone. There was a strong wind blowing, and it had started to snow. It was the fifth time I had taken his route and I knew the road quite well. There were yaks, as always, in both directions. It was very cold. My rucksack was lighter this time because I had left my down-filled clothes at the Advance Camp last week so I wouldn't have to carry them. I hoped I wouldn't die of cold tonight and tomorrow without them. I walked fast and tensely. I no longer admired the scenery because I knew it. I only rested at one place above the Tibetan camp where there was a shelter from the wind. It was my favourite place to relax with wonderful scenery. At one point the snow got stronger, but didn't accumulate. The wind scattered it. It took me four hours to reach Intermediate Camp. As always, the camp manager was alone and I would spend the evening in his company. I tried to argue with him because he had slept in my bag and smoked cigarettes in it. But he didn't understand a word I was saying to him. I think he finally got the message and I hoped that when I left it in storage again tomorrow, he wouldn't sleep in it again. Today would be the third time I had slept at the Intermediate Camp at 5,800 metres.

It was snowing at the camp and it was freezing. I went into my tent and tucked myself into my sleeping bag to keep warm. When I'd warmed up a bit, I went to Sambo's tent to ask him to cook something for me. There was almost nothing left, and some spaghetti in packets.

A View of Chomolungma from Base Camp, 5200 metres

He boiled some water and put the spaghetti in it. There was nothing else to eat. It was a good job I had brought some of my newly discovered provisions and ate some of them. After dinner I went to bed to rest and gather strength. I was still angry about the food ... What's the point of locking the stable door after the horse has ? But I was happy as well. I had no idea how long I would be staying at Base Camp. When I got back to Base Camp on May 8, I would eat the nuts and dried fruit. The dates were a little like stone, but they were edible.

The Chinese Base Camp and The First Vegan on Everest.

Day 30

Waking up in the Intermediate Camp at 5800 metres.

5 May 2014

The wind blew and blew all night long, only abating slightly in the morning. It wasn't very cold, and I was used to it anyway. There was about five inches of snow on the ground. As they say "Winter caught us unawares again." I put my sleeping bag outside for a while to dry in the sun. Because of the condensation in the morning, the bag was always damp around the opening for the head where the warm and cold air met. I packed my bags, and Sambo made me tea and pancakes for breakfast. When I say pancakes, I don't mean typical pancakes, but a dough-like concoction without eggs or milk. I ate a couple with some leftover old jam and drank two cups of tea. I packed the sleeping bag and warned him not to sleep in it anymore. I left it in the cooking tent wrapped in two plastic bags and squeezed into a corner. I hope he didn't touch it. Later I realized that it was common practice for the Sherpas to sleep in the bags of the climbers, so as not to use their own. Strange people, but you can't do without them.

I left the Intermediate Camp following some yaks that soon disappeared into the distance ahead of me. I walked slowly to save energy. The next day I planned to go to sleep at Camp 1 - North Col, 7100 metres. The wind was blowing at my back, which was better than blowing in my face. On the way I bumped into Viktor who hadn't found a new client and was finally leaving for Russia. He was just waiting for the yaks to bring his equipment down to Base Camp, as well as that of Alexander. Then I met the two Indians who had gone up to Camp 1 yesterday without sleeping there. Bill had also been up there without sleeping. Then I met the two Poles who had slept the day before in Camp 1. I stopped to rest, to eat a protein bar in the usual rest place with the tent.

About an hour before Advanced Base Camp, I was walking in the tracks left by yaks and other climbers in the ice and snow. The path went around a lake. I could see that the snow and ice underfoot was soft and melted, but other people had been that way before me. The moment I stepped onto the frozen lake, my left leg fell into the water up to my thigh. It was real bad luck that my whole leg was soaked. I didn't have any clean socks or plastic bags to change into. It was bad. I had three-season boots but after three years of service and countless miles, the Goretex wasn't waterproof. I had no other option but to get to the camp as quickly as possible and change my boots. It was well below zero and my leg could freeze. I quickened my pace to prevent this from happening. Within about 45 minutes I reached the Advance Base Camp for the third time in this expedition. I get into my tent as quick as I could and changed into warm socks. Then I filled a bottle with hot water and wrapped myself up in my sleeping bag to get warm. I just hoped I didn't get sick, that would be all I needed. I also took an aspirin to warm myself up and even began to sweat. Then I had dinner alone and chatted to my Sherpa about tomorrow. He didn't want to go up with me because he had come up yesterday to transport luggage to the Advance Base Camp and he was tired. I explained to him that this was my last chance to ascend and sleep there because the weather forecast in two days' time was for long-term deterioration of the weather for at least a week. He eventually agreed to go with me. Up until this point I had only used his services to go to Camp 1 the previous week. I went to bed in the tent after dinner and thought about what I should do. I already had slept five nights at this altitude - 6440 metres - and I hoped to get a good night's sleep.

DAY 31

May 6, St. George's Day at the Bulgarian Calendar

From day 11 to day 32

The night was calm and I slept well, except for the obligatory visits to the toilet and drinking water. The morning was quiet, calm and sunny, with a beautiful view of the top.

I felt it would be a good day. It was St. George's Day after all, and my father's name day, which we celebrate in Bulgaria. A name day is celebrated, as far as I am aware, in Bulgaria and other southern, central, and eastern European countries as a tradition similar to a birthday. At breakfast, to honour my father's name day, I gave all the Sherpas organic bars that I brought from Bulgaria. The treat gift is another custom in Bulgaria that you give to your close friends and loved ones at your special moments such as birthday or name day.

After breakfast, I decided not to use the Batura double-layered boots I had worn to climb to Camp 1 the previous time, but test the triple-layered boots I would attack the top with. I also decided to try the down-filled overalls I had bought in Kathmandu. It would be like a dress rehearsal with clothes and boots for the final march to the Roof of the World, which I hoped would take place by May 16 or 17.

It's very important to test all your equipment in the mountains and know what to expect. So I put on my overalls and the Olympus boots to test them along the North Col route. Olympus aren't as technical and light as the Batura, but they're life-saving. I pulled on the overalls and put on the triple-layered boots I hadn't worn since January 5 when I descended from Camp 2 - Nido de Condores to Aconcagua to Plaza de Mulas (Base Camp). I was used to walking with these boots and I felt good. However, it was so sunny and warm that as soon as I left the Advance Camp, I started sweating. I left on my own and agreed to meet Gilgen at Crampon Spot (where we put on our crampons on) because the Sherpas were allocating the high-altitude food among themselves. I told Gilgen to take only spaghetti for me, I didn't want any Toblerones, chocolates, meat, or cheese.

I started my ascent and felt very hot. I unzipped the top part of overalls and tied it around my waist. I opened all its vents as well. But it wasn't much use. Gilgen caught up with me at Crampon Spot. Here I decided to take off my overalls and walk in my thermal underwear. A very wise decision, given that it was so hot and I was burning up in the sun and snow. We attached the seats and the crampons that were waiting for us.

We went to the familiar place at the beginning of the guide rope. At the beginning of the guide rope we took the usual break for something sweet to eat. The heat was merciless. Very high temperature and very strong solar radiation, without a hint of a wind. I felt weak, without an ounce of strength, but the wall was still waiting to be climbed by us. At the beginning of the wall we met some Austrians who were going to climb it for the first time. Like I did the last time, I left one of my sticks, hooked the Jumara to the guide rope, secured the handle with a carabineer, and began to pull myself up on the Jumara and push on my legs. The sun was beating down on us. According to the forecast, it should have been cold and stormy.

It was definitely a more difficult climb today than it was a week ago. First, my shoes were heavier and bulkier, second, my rucksack was heavier because of the sleeping bag, and third, the sun was exhausting. Apart from the sleeping bag in my rucksack, I was carrying a blanket, the down-filled overalls I had taken off, and some other things. We climbed slowly and steadily. There wasn't anyone else ahead of us, but it wasn't the pace of the previous time. We took frequent breaks for air which was scarce here. About midway up the wall, the sky suddenly darkened, the sun disappeared for literally two minutes and it started snowing. In the space of less than five minutes the temperature fell from plus 30 degrees to minus 10-15. It was like jumping into a cold pool after a sauna. I immediately pulled my overalls out of my rucksack and it was all I could do to put them on over my boots without taking them off. It was a good thing the zippers opened wide enough. I was glad that I had something branded and high quality, albeit second hand.

It began to snow really heavily. We continued up in the snow, eventually catching up with David and his Sherpa, who had planned to sleep at Camp 2 at 7,700 metres the night before. David could barely move and had no strength. How on earth would he get to 8848 metres. I had no idea.

On the one hand, it was a good thing that I saw what it was like to climb without oxygen, but on the other hand, everybody is individual and reacts differently to altitude. There was no guarantee that I would react so badly. I had already decided to use oxygen, I had even arranged it. There was no point in taking any chances. Due to a number of factors, but most of all the tragic avalanche that had cost the lives of so many innocent people, but the constant theatricals of the rest of the group and the lack of correspondence between words and deeds, I didn't see any point in climbing to the Roof of the World without oxygen, as I had originally intended.

The previous clarity of motivation which I formulated while leading a normal life in civilization, was now blurred against the power and greatness of Mother Nature in a world dominated by the struggle for mental and physical survival. David couldn't say a word. He was unable even to speak, although I still felt well at this altitude and in good condition. We continued up the steep slopes, my rucksack was very heavy and I was panting. The thick snow was making the going even harder. The climb today was beautiful, absolutely fitting for St. George's Day. Mysterious, enigmatic, spiritual and full of love, entirely fitting for an Everest expedition.

At one point, the snow-covered tents of the camp appeared. We had arrived safely at Camp 1 North Col at 7,100 metres. I couldn't believe I'd made it today. This climb had been the most difficult physical activity in my life so far ... Or at least that's how it seemed. It really pumped my muscles up and at one point I didn't even believe we would make it. I found the wall very difficult this time. It took an hour longer to climb it this time, but in the mountains, it doesn't matter how long it takes, what matters is to climb it to the top. And most of all that you get back down safe and sound. I consider myself a very sensible and cautious person, not prepared to take unnecessary risks. I do only what I know to be safe, but still there has to be a certain amount of courage and confidence. Without courage, confidence, perseverance, faith, concentration and will-power, you can't climb a mountain in such conditions.

I was so happy that I'd made it to here. I was as tired and thirsty as a Bedouin. It was a good thing Gilgen had come up two days previously and pitched our tent. It was covered in snow. Heavy snow had fallen on Camp 1 and was still accumulating. More than one metre of snow. Only the roof of the tent was visible and we dug out the tent with a shovel. We shook the snow off ourselves. I went inside to rest, while my Sherpa went to get hot tea from the special tent, where they melted large quantities of snow on a large gas stove. Over the past two hours, I drank over a litre and a half of water and I had not peed yet, even though 8 hours had passed since the morning. I recalled that when I climbed to Camp 3 at an altitude of 6,100 metres on Mount Lenin, I had to drink water for two hours before I was able to pee. I was 1000 metres higher up here. Every time I exhaled, I expelled moisture from my body. I began to feel better, removed the snow off our tent and went to eat with Gilgen in the common tent. I felt well. I was incredibly tired, and exhausted, but I didn't have a headache or any other health complaints. Yesterday I had diarrhoea and today I ate only two slices of bread for breakfast, but now everything was fine. I had found this climb with my equipment and the heavy backpack terribly difficult. Now that I think about it, it would have been easier for me with the double-layered boots, and just the down-filled jacket. However, over the last three years in the mountains I had learned that equipment had to be tested before a serious climb. So it was important to try these overalls and the triple-layered boots today.

We boiled up some spaghetti for dinner. There were about six or seven Sherpas from our expedition in the kitchen tent. They had come up to Camp 1 today to deliver oxygen bottles, more tents for the upper camps, and food. Their clients had gone down the day before. They cooked the spaghetti and served me first, and then they added meat. The spaghetti was so spicy that I thought they wanted to poison me. I adore spicy food, but theirs was almost impossible to eat. But I was so hungry I ate it.

It was still light when I went to bed in the tent, and it minus 5 degrees. I couldn't imagine how cold it would get during the night. Gilgen and I talked about the next day. Our plan was to climb 100-200 metres up towards Camp 2 and descend to Advance Base Camp. The weather was forecast to be bad. I definitely felt fatigued. Today marked a month since I had left Sliven. Tonight would be the first time in my life that I would sleep at 7100 metres above sea level. Miracles happen. Who would have believed it that I would have made it this far in less than three years.

The temperature in the tent began to drop gradually. I couldn't sleep, and every 30 minutes or so I kept track of the time and the temperature like a meteorologist. The snow was thick outside and it was still snowing. There was maybe a metre of fresh snow. After those spicy spaghetti, I needed to use the toilet. What was I going to do now? I didn't know the zips on the back of the overalls yet. It was a good job I had Goretex trousers and a thin Goretex jacket. I got dressed, but it was already minus 15 degrees outside and snowing heavily. Where was I going to find a toilet? Ten metres or so from the tent towards the overhang, I dug a hole, did what I had to do, buried it like a cat and returned to the tent. The sky was beautiful and filled with stars. It took me half an hour to regain my body temperature. I was glad I had a good sleeping bag which quickly warmed me.

Two days ago I had ordered three bottles of oxygen and a mask with a regulator. People normally use six or seven bottles for Everest. There were exceptions, like Bill, who wanted to sleep for two nights in Camp 3 at 8,300 metres, and he had ordered twelve bottles and two Sherpas to help him. The Indians had seven bottles each, everyone else had six bottles, and only David had no oxygen. I had heard that in 2004, the climbers had used 11 bottles when climbing Everest.

The northern wall of Everest, Tibet

Day 32

May 7 2014

During the night the temperatures in the tent dropped to minus 20. I didn't feel cold in my bag. I was completely wrapped up with only a small hole left for air. It's impossible to sleep at this altitude. I dozed off slight from time to time, but I may not have slept at all. My body itched all over. I don't know if it that was due to the lack of oxygen, but I tossed and turned constantly. At 4.30 in the morning, Gilgen and I were wide awake and decided to get up, eat something, and pack. We poured warm water over our muesli, and I added some nuts.

Walking from Camp 1 to Camp 2

I had a good appetite and ate everything. So at 5.30 there was no one outside, and we were already walking towards Camp 2.

We walked for about an hour along the guide rope to which we were hooked up with our Jumara and reached 7250 metres. This was the end of my acclimatization and my altitude record so far in my life. I was ready to make my attempt on the top using oxygen. My decision was final and had come about as a combination of many things: my food had disappeared, and I had been eating only carbohydrates for a month, David had struggled seven times to climb without oxygen and looked atrocious, I lacked experience and didn't know what awaited me. Everest wasn't going away, it would always be here and I could always come back again and try without oxygen. It was important to reach the top and get back down safe and sound.

Gilgen pointed out to me a number of peaks in Nepal that were visible from the northern edge, as well as the border between Nepal and Tibet, west of the peak. It looked like something out of a fairy tale, I could see the whole wall in front of me, I mean the North Wall. We drank tea and admired the view. We had no rucksacks, we had only taken a flask of tea. Such incredible beauty ... I couldn't take my eyes off it despite the strong wind from the east. To the north of Camp 1 stands Changtse Peak at 7553 metres. It's so beautiful and fascinating. After admiring the scenery, we headed back to Camp 1. We packed our bags and went down again. We were the first to go back down that day. It was always much quicker going down the wall. The snow was virgin, no one had passed yet. I felt exhausted by the lack of sleep in Camp 1. I had two bottles of oxygen next to me all night, and I wondered what it would be like to breathe oxygen, I had never tried, but I resisted the temptation.

In less than 45 minutes we were at the base of the wall. It was a wonderful, unique sunny day with beautiful views of the Advance Base Camp. I retrieved the stick I had left at the base of the wall the day before and we walked over the glacier to the barrels to leave our seats, crampons and other equipment. By around 10.30 we were already in the Advance Base Camp, 6440 metres. I was as hungry as a wolf and ate what I found in the tent. I went to bed and, as they say, felt like a dead man. I wanted to sleep, but couldn't. I wanted to go down to Base Camp, but I didn't think I had the strength to walk for 8 hours. I rested for about an hour without sleeping and went to lunch. It occurred to me that instead of staying at 6440 metres and struggling, it would be better if I went straight down directly to Base Camp. No sooner said than done.

In ten minutes I had packed my bags and at 13.45 I started down the Heracles highway. The Sherpas wondered whether I would make it, as I had descended from 7250 metres today, and I hadn't slept. What they didn't know was that my specialty was walking for hours on end over huge distances. When I walk, I rest more than dosing in the tent. So full speed ahead, I felt as if I was flying. In less than two and a half hours, I reached the Intermediate Camp all by myself. I flew all the way. I just retrieved my sleeping bag from Sambo's tent, he wasn't there, and I didn't even look for him. Without eating anything, I continued to Base Camp.

With every metre of descent, I felt better from the higher oxygen content in the air. By

18.35 I was back in the Base Camp. I had covered the distance of 25km in less than 5 hours, and I had descended to the Front Base Camp, from 7250 metres, all in one day. In other words, I had descended 2000 metres and covered over 30 kilometres. I was right on time for dinner. I even went to the officer to ask if anyone was going down to Tingri the next day so I could go and rest. Everyone else was already in Tingri except David, who had returned to Base Camp a few hours before me today. The officer told me that Viktor, the Russian, was travelling to Zangmu tomorrow. My eyes widened in surprise. That would be even better if I could go down to 2300 metres. The officer asked me how much money I could give him to take me to Zangmu for two nights in the jeep. I couldn't believe my ears. That's what I had been wanting all day. Tomorrow I would be in Zangmu, 2300 metres. I knew the jeep cost $ 920 one way. I offered him $ 200 for both directions, because the jeep would be coming back anyway. We shook hands and agreed that I would be ready to leave at 10 o'clock. We agreed on two nights in Zangmu. I returned to our camp for dinner. Viktor was sleeping in his tent. The others told me that he had drunk a few bottles of vodka with the other Russians at lunch in the Russian camp and had barely recovered. He was crawling on all fours and vomiting like a geyser. I decided there was no point in waking him up. I had dinner and went to bed. I thanked the Goddess for being so kind to me. Not only did I get back down to

Base Camp unscathed today, but she had rewarded me with a rest at the lowest possible place in Tibet. The force was with me and I could feel it with all my senses, receptors, heart and soul. Whatever you really wish for, it comes true. I fell asleep like a baby and didn't get up in the night to drink water.

Happy at Base Camp

The magnetic peak Chomolungma

From day 33 to day 44

DAY 33

May 8, 2014

A wonderful sunny morning. Of course, there was a strong wind, but who cared about the wind in Base Camp? I was so happy that my acclimatization was over. I was alive and well, and most importantly, I was going to be able to descend to 2300 metres above sea level. I had been at such a low altitude for a month. It's essential before the final trek to the top for the body to rest and replenish its oxygen. I would only spend two nights in Zangmu, but that was enough, especially given that the cost of transportation is extortionate. One night's accommodation and food in Zangmu is $100 per person per day. So I needed to spend another $200. Well, that was the last of the money and I had decided to invest in my respite. Anyway, there was point in holding on to it.

Although I've never run out of money wherever I've been, I've always kept some in reserve.

Viktor appeared at breakfast. He had a massive headache from the vodka the day before. I told him that I had talked to the officer and that we would be travelling to Zangmu together. He was a bit slow to react, but he nodded. The others in the group, with the exception of David, had already gone down to Tingri to rest. I didn't intend to take much luggage. It was only two nights and the journey took hours. I was glad that the nuts and dried fruits had been returned and I took them with me, although I would buy fresh fruits and vegetables at the market in Zangmu. I took some clothes to wash the dust off them.

Viktor prepared Alex's eight bags and his own two or three. The minibus with the officer inside arrived. He was going to make the most of the chance to go down to rest in Zangmu. It was a good job it was a big minibus, otherwise we wouldn't have been able to load up all those huge bags.

The driver drove slowly to Tingri, we weren't in a jeep after all. I knew the road well ... there wasn't much of interest to see. The only site of note just before Tingri on the right is a hill on which there is a fortress, and the remains are still visible. Cho Oyu can also be seen well in good weather.

When we reached Tingri, we took a break for lunch at the restaurant where I had been last week, and then headed to Zangmu. The distance from Tingri to Zangmu is about 140 km, along tarred roads. It was a pleasant two-way panoramic road. There wasn't much traffic. After Tingri, they give you a note showing what time you crossed the checkpoint and you are not allowed to arrive in Nyalam in less than two hours. We reached the pass at 5000 metres and got out of the minibus to admire the amazing views. Then there was a steep descent to Nyalam. We passed through many villages with the Chinese flag flying on the houses. We would have arrived too early at Nyalam, so we stopped for half an hour. There was plenty of vegetation here, and I enjoyed every green plant I saw.

We didn't enter Nyalam, but continued on to Zangmu on the

border with Nepal. The lower we went, the greener it became, and with my whole body, heart and mind I could sense the higher oxygen content in the air. It was good. I could feel enormous strength coming to my arms and legs. My lungs were filled with oxygen, it was an incredible feeling. It was already dark before we reached Zangmu, and I realised that we had been travelling for seven hours. A long journey, but worth it.

The moment I got out of the minibus in Zangmu, I felt as if I had just been born! I couldn't get enough of the oxygen and the greenery. Now I understand why Alex left for London after going to Zangmu last week. Before we checked into the hotel, Victor and I sat down to dinner, the trip had made us hungry. Until now I had not drunk beer during the entire expedition, but today I decided to have one, Lhasa, of course. They also brought me a salad with fresh vegetables, which I gladly accepted. They made me rice with vegetables and Nepalese tofu. The owner of the restaurant was Nepalese.

After dinner, Victor and I parted and never saw each other again. He wanted to leave for Kathmandu early in the morning. I took a private room in the luxury hotel and before taking a shower, I decided to wash my clothes. There was plenty of hot water. I stopped by the window from time to time to admire the huge green trees and the fresh air. I just have no words to describe the feelings I was feeling at that moment, after a month at an altitude of more than 5200 metres and without greenery. Every breath of air I took brought me the most incredible pleasure! I could feel the oxygen moving in my blood and reaching every cell in my body and brain. The high oxygen level revived me so strongly that I didn't feel in the least tired. I washed everything and took a bath. It was too late to wash my hair and I decided to do it the next day.

I was lying in bed with white sheets and a comfortable mattress. The room temperature was 20 degrees. Life was wonderful.

Base camp and the "mother ship"

DAY 34

May 9 2014

Zangmu, 2300 metres, the border with Nepal The most delicious salad

I slept soundly all night. In the morning the sun woke me. I was in no hurry to get up. I was in no hurry to go anywhere. I had no plans or jobs to do today, apart from relaxing as much as possible and gather oxygen for the top. I got up and what did I see from the window. Green, green, green, green ... This is the most beautiful colour you can possibly wish for after a month at altitude.

For me there was nothing more wonderful than being among green trees. The oxygen was a unique sensation, I felt it so strongly. I could hear birds singing, and I ate an apple at the window admiring the endless greenery. I could hear the torrenting river. I went down to the restaurant to eat something fresh and delicious. I ordered a fruit and vegetable salad and, of course, green tea. I had never eaten such a salad before. It was made of cucumbers, radishes, bananas, apples, carrots, beets and other fruits and vegetables. It was so delicious and fresh. Zangmu has terraced gardens and greenhouses for growing vegetables. It was the best season of the year for them right now. After the salad, I ate some spaghetti.

After breakfast, I decided to go for a walk. The town is made up a single 10 km long street with a difference in altitude of 500 metres from one end to the other. I went up to have a look around. I was told that there were hot mineral water springs, but they were 20 km from the city and I needed a special permit ...So I discounted the mineral pool from my plans. I took a walk and looked at the shops. They sold everything here. I shopped for all kinds of fresh fruit. I also found a post office and wondered if I should send cards to Bulgaria, but I just bought them without sending them. The cards from Kilimanjaro never actually arrived, and from Aconcagua they arrived two months late. After the market I went back to my room to rest for a while and it started to rain pleasantly. The air became even fresher. I rested and couldn't stop delighting in the natural surroundings and eating all kinds of fruits. Then I thought about how beautiful Bulgaria is. How green the mountains still are, and here, at an altitude of over 4000 metres, there's nothing but , stones, rocks, sand, snow, ice and cold. I personally prefer to be amongst vegetation, rather than in desert and lunar landscapes over 5000 metres.

Nepalese-Tibetan vegan lunch

I felt hungry again and went to the restaurant to order something tasty. I ordered a combination menu that included as much rice as you could eat, lettuce, potatoes and very spicy lentils. There was also Nepalese spicy bread - very thin flat, crispy bread.

The rain continued to fall softly and gently, watering Mother Nature. I took a shower and washed my hair. This time it had been much less than 26 days since I last washed it.

I continued to fill my lungs at the window, replenishing my body with oxygen. I sliced a delicious mango. I rested in my room until dinner. I was making plans for how I would return to Base Camp tomorrow, then ascend to the top on May 11. If the Force allowed, I would reach the summit on May 16 or 17. You can't make plans about mountains if not there; plans are made in the mountains, but since I had nothing else to do, I dreamed of reaching the peak. I missed my loved ones very much ...

I had never been on such a long expedition before, and the end was nowhere near yet. The important thing was that I was healthy, happy and full of love. I was flying!

Day 35

May 10, 2014

The two nights and the day in Zangmu passed quickly. I didn't really feel like going back to Base Camp, but I had an important mission to accomplish. If I see a point to something, I always make sure I finish. This was the most meaningful thing I had ever done in my life. I wanted to test the limits of veganism. I wanted to see if it really worked. If more people discovered veganism and experienced it, then fewer animals would be bred for slaughter, and the environment would be less be polluted. The mission was clear, precise and blessed.

I slept well again, and the birds woke me up with their morning chorus. I was in heaven. I stood at the window and took a deep breath of morning energy. I wanted to breathe in all the air. After breakfast I had some time left before we went back to Base Camp, so I decided to take a walk down the street. It was a nice, sunny day. I took photographs of people who had no idea where I was going.

The officer was late for breakfast, and I waited for him to show up. The driver would be the same Tibetan from last week with the broken-down Toyota. I wasn't very happy, but I had no choice. They said it had been repaired. There was another person with us. He was the manager of the T-shop before Base Camp. They went to do some shopping for the Base Camp and we spent another hour in Zangmu ... But what was I in a hurry for? On the way back we headed into Tingri. After an hour or so, there wasn't a trace of the beautiful greenery left. Today I would go from 2300 metres to 5200 metres altitude in the space of a few hours. An ascent of almost 3000 metres. I hoped the avatar held up. There was green tea for breakfast, but I didn't feel like drinking it, so I poured the petals and all into my thermos flask for the trip.

About two hours later we arrived in Nyalam and the officer decided to stop for something to eat. I had eaten here last month and the chef recognized me. Without saying a word, he made me a delicious vegan work of art. Again without taking the cigarette out of his mouth, he fried the vegetables for me in a matter of seconds. Whatever I ate in these latitudes was delicious.

After Nyalam we were given the note with the time of arrival, and our driver was very angry. He liked to drive fast and not adhere to the rules of the People's Republic of China. After crossing the pass and descending into the lowlands, we realized that we were 40 minutes early and had to rest. The sun was shining and a very strong wind was blowing. After all, we were at an altitude of 4,500 metres. The driver stopped the car by a river, got a towel and some soap, and headed for the river. We were just beyond the turning for Shishapangma peak. I didn't get out of the car because I could feel the strong wind through my hat, and my head was freezing. Despite the freezing temperatures, the Tibetan driver washed his hair with soap in the river and then sat on the grass to drink tea. Such a thing I had never seen before. He could have reached the top without down-filled clothes and a hat.

Chomolungma and Cho Oyu together, just before Tingri

Just before Tingri, the most beautiful view of Chomolungma and Cho Oyu appears.

We rested for about half hour, then we headed to Tingri, where we ate again quickly and left for Base Camp. My plan was to spend one day at the most there, and perhaps even go straight to Advance Base Camp the next day. However, it is one thing to think and dream, reality is quite another thing. Over the last three days, I hadn't bothered checking the weather forecast for the next few days. In order to reach the top, you have to leave Base Camp a week in advance, and there are a total of six camps at the top. Even if the weather is bad up to Camp 3, the most important thing is to have good weather on the day of the final ascent.

I arrived at the Base Camp, and what did I see? None of the members were there, and all the Sherpas were at Base Camp. I realized something was wrong. I was immediately informed to my surprise that for the next five or six or even seven days, any ascent to the top would be out of the question. The forecast was for very bad weather, and the Chinese hadn't yet installed the guide rope from 8300 metres to the top. So why had I come back? I could have stayed in Tingri with the others for a couple of more days, ... but I forgot, I had no more money ... The money I had spent on two days in Zangmu, I could have had 5 days in Tingri. But I didn't regret it at all ... Zangmu was a paradise, and my trip had cost me much less than the usual exorbitant prices. No one gives you invoices, receipts, or anything like that.

There was a strong hurricane-force wind blowing at the Advance Base Camp, and everyone had descended. At Camp 1 the tents were flying through the air. The wind at the summit was over 120 km per hour.

At Base Camp, the wind was also record-breaking, but at least there was a nice view of the top. I felt a little sad that I would have to lie here dozing for at least a week. There was supposed to be a window around May 17-18, but there was no guide rope to the top.

It would the 18th at least before the group that installed it could get up there. I was trapped. But whatever... Waiting for a window was also part of the expedition.

After a while, the Indians and Richard turned up. Only Kristiano, Billy and David were still in Tingri. After dinner I went to bed with mixed feelings. I had so much strength and energy.

From May 11 to May 18

2014

The week wasn't just long, but infinitely long, cold, windy and almost monotonous. Every single day there was a very strong wind, completely unsuitable for walking. You get up in the morning, and have breakfast in the shared tent. Then you either stay here or go back to your own tent. The other members of our expedition returned after their few days rest in Tingri. I wanted to walk around Base Camp at least, but the wind blew through my zips and clothes and froze my entire body. I thought to myself, I come from a windy area myself, but this was a wind to end all winds.

I had brought nothing to read with me, and I desperately wanted to read. So I borrowed the two books on Everest that Kristian ocopied his notes from every day, as if they were his own thoughts and discoveries. So I started reading them, or rather looking at the pictures and trying to make head or tail of the Polish. I could understand certain things from the context, others from the pictures. The pictures were very good. Both books were about the Nepalese route to Everest. I spent a couple of hours looking at them, and then returned them to him so he could continue copying them out of his internet site and his sponsors. The others had laptops and surfed the net or watched movies on them. While I meditated alone in the tent. I liked to spend the first hour huddled up in my warm sleeping bag, dozing and thinking about life and its laws and rules. Then when I got bored of that I wanted to get to the top, and all this confusion about the weather forecast just affected me psychologically. It was so boring and just a huge waste of time, for me at least. There are many people who like to take it easy and rest, but if there's one thing I don't like, it's doing nothing and wasting my time. If only I had something to write with. I could write a whole book. It wasn't exactly true that I wasting my time. It would have been just too easy, to get acclimatized and then get straight to the top in good weather. I had to learn to be patient, I needed it. After my previous expeditions I had an idea what it was like to be patient, but ten days... that was a personal record. As I was writing the word "record," I recalled a few more records that I had set myself for this expedition.

Prayers inscribed on stones

Every couple of hours we received information about the weather forecast. Most of the other members had paid for text messages with the weather forecast to be sent to them. Of course, that was an option I hadn't paid for and I didn't receive any text messages or emails, or no one called me on the satellite phone. Kaloyan Ganev once called me, and that made me very happy. Hardly anyone knew my number. Only my closest family and friends, in fact. It cost 6 Euros per minute for someone from Bulgaria or anywhere in the world to call me.

Bill was the one who received the most information from a meteorological service in the United States. It was after all Bill's fifth expedition to the Roof of the World and he had paid for a special subscription to the forecast. The forecast was far from encouraging, even suggesting an extended period of bad weather. David also received forecasts from Hungary, but he didn't like to share them. There wasn't much he did like, apart from Johnny Walker, cigars and red wine. A real know-it-all, but I neither envied him, wondered about him, and least of all mocked him. I imagine it can't have been easy for him, particularly from a psychological point of view, coming seven times in a row and still not being welcomed with open arms by Goddess. I hoped at least he would get home safe and sound. I imagined he had close family who were waiting for him. David told us all he was a "gypsy" and very proud of it. He was the leader of some Roma organizations in Hungary and even at European level. He didn't actually have any day to day job, of course.

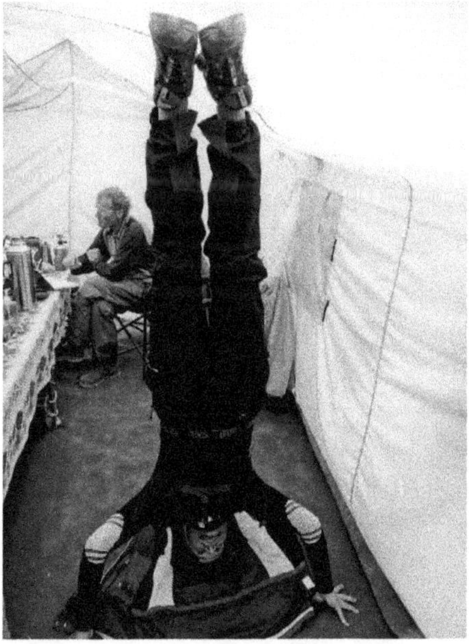

Keeping fit in the shared tent, Base camp, 5200 metres

On May 13, the first meeting took place between all the expeditions and the Chinese Tibetan Mountain Service. They were in charge of organising everything, including the installation of the guide rope from North Col to the top. The meeting took place in the Mountain Service's own huge tent, and all the companies attended. First they argued, then they laughed ... It didn't really matter anyway. All the companies had taken their clients' money whether they got to the top or not. The most important thing, in any case, was not to risk your life. For every organizer the most important thing was not to put lives at risk and avoid casualties. There was no chance at the moment of anyone going up the mountainside in the next few days, especially without a guide rope. They agreed to meet again in two days' time to discuss the situation.

The general meeting at Base Camp during the "Window". All expeditions in attendance.

Rong Pu Old Monastery, 5000 metres

When the meeting was over, I decided to visit the old Rong Pu Monastery close to Base Camp. It had burned down many years ago, and then a new one was built about three kilometres further down. I passed it several times already, and I wanted to take a closer look. There was still a strong wind blowing and it was absolutely freezing. But I had made my mind up to go there.

I set out in the roaring wind and made slow progress. There's a shortcut over the big bends in the road and avoids any danger of being run over by a car or bus. The monastery is just before the T-shop. It's raised above the road and you have to climb a flight of cement steps to the entrance. It was so very beautiful. A whole complex of buildings, stupas, flags, and prayer mills. I looked around and took photographs and video.

There wasn't a living soul to be seen, even a yak wouldn't have endured the cold. I found an entrance and slipped into a half-closed room which was brighter than the light of the sun. A huge number of lighted candles and candlesticks were arranged on a large table. The room was so warm that I even took my jacket off. It was such an astonishing place, so cosy and warm, full of intimate energy, so pleasant ... I couldn't believe where I was. I began to examine everything in the room carefully. I immediately noticed that in the ground next to the table there was a sixty-by-eighty-centimetre opening through which another room could be seen below. It was also filled with bright light and a pleasant fragrance. With just a single leap, I descended to the lower level through the narrow gap. I'm curious by nature and have a thirst for knowledge. It was the main room, or perhaps the altar in their understanding. Here again, there were many burning candles, statues of various deities, photographs and money left by worshippers.

Rong Pu Old Monastery, upper level, main prayer hall

The lower level of the old Rong Pu Monastery

It was quite unbelievable, it was as if someone had been expecting me and lit all these candles just for me. There wasn't a soul to be seen. The ceiling in this underground level was quite low and you can't walk upright. There are niches in the walls containing religious symbols and objects. They're impossible to enter, especially if you're overweight. I liked it so much I stayed here for a while. I felt wonderful and could feel my avatar being charged with energy and my soul with love. I went back to look at the upper level, and then went down again for a while. There are no stairs between the two levels, just a stone you use as a step and you pull yourself up using your arm muscles. A wonderful altar - I immediately thought about our Orthodox priests and bishops. They were all so well-fed so that if they had to try and squeeze in here, they would have to give up their sweet service to the name of God. Of course, I also remembered the cave of St. Ivan Rilski and its narrow entrance, which any well-fed priest would have difficulty getting through. It's impossible.

My first visit to Tibet was in 2010 when I had visited the sacred lake Nam Tso. Next to the lake there's a rock formation shaped like a twisted funnel. It's very narrow, and the locals believe that you can only squeeze through the gap if you are without sin. The entire world seems to live by the rule that overeating is sinful.

I must have spent more than an hour walking around the monastery. I went into every nook and cranny but didn't come across a living soul. I found signs of life in one room. There was dried meat hanging on the walls and lots of candles burning, but the person who lived in the room was nowhere to be seen. It was either the guardian of the monastery or a monk.

The wind was getting up, so I headed back to the Chinese base camp, about an hour's walk from the old Rong Pu Monastery.

I don't want to dwell in detail on what happened every day, just the more important things, like a very nasty argument that almost ended in a fight. Every evening in the shared tent, a gas burner is lit for about one hour during dinner. One of the Indians decided to turn it down, but ended up breaking it, and it stopped working. So I told him not to touch things he didn't understand, and that because of him we would have to put up with the cold. We started arguing and calling each other names, to the point that we almost ended up in a fight. We were clearly all on edge. No one had any idea whether the weather would be suitable for an ascent. Good weather was forecast for after the third of June, and then the monsoons began.

As cold as it was, I tried to keep fit every day either in the shared tent or in my own. My tent was too low for exercising, and I couldn't do anything but stretch in a sitting position. In the shared tent, I could do a variety of exercises and headstands which is my favourite exercise for concentration. The others looked at me strangely when I did my gymnastics. I wasn't disturbing anyone, the tent was quite big enough for everyone to do whatever they wanted. The Poles played chess, the Indians watched movies, while the Hungarians had their own huge heated tent.

They preferred to stay there rather than gather with the common people. Bill stayed in his own tent, only coming out for food.

One morning I decided to go for a longer walk. I took my rucksack, some water and food, and headed up the road along a river, which was sheltered from the cold wind. The ice had melted much more in the past month since we had arrived. As I walked up the river, the ice crackled under my feet. It even broke in several places, but I was lucky not to fall through. I walked for about two or three hours and felt great.

On May 16, I asked Bill for one of his books. It was a 1928 book that described the first Everest expeditions, including Mallory's on the Tibetan side. The route I had taken was described in detail, but 90 years ago. I admired these real men who had no modern equipment, planes, or logistics. It took them months to reach Rong Pu Monastery and months to return. Such an expedition then lasted six to seven months. They had no idea where they were going and how they would make the climb. They were great people in every respect. Such an interesting book. The camps they set up then are still used today to climb Mount Chomolungma from Tibet.

I'm inclined personally to believe that Mallory managed to reach the top. A few years ago, his body was found just beneath the summit. The photo of his wife, which he wanted to leave at the top, was missing. People had different morals and value system. They were nothing like the current professional climbers who exaggerate everything about the mountains. There's no sportsmanship, collegiality, or respect. It is such a pity that they have turned the mountain into big business. From what I heard and discovered in recent days is that they even lie about climbing mountains they've never been to. Is this how low mountaineering has sunk? I don't want to be part of a group of such fake people and society. As far as I'm concerned, the mountain and the peaks are sacred places. If the mountain doesn't allow to me reach its peak, then now is not the time.

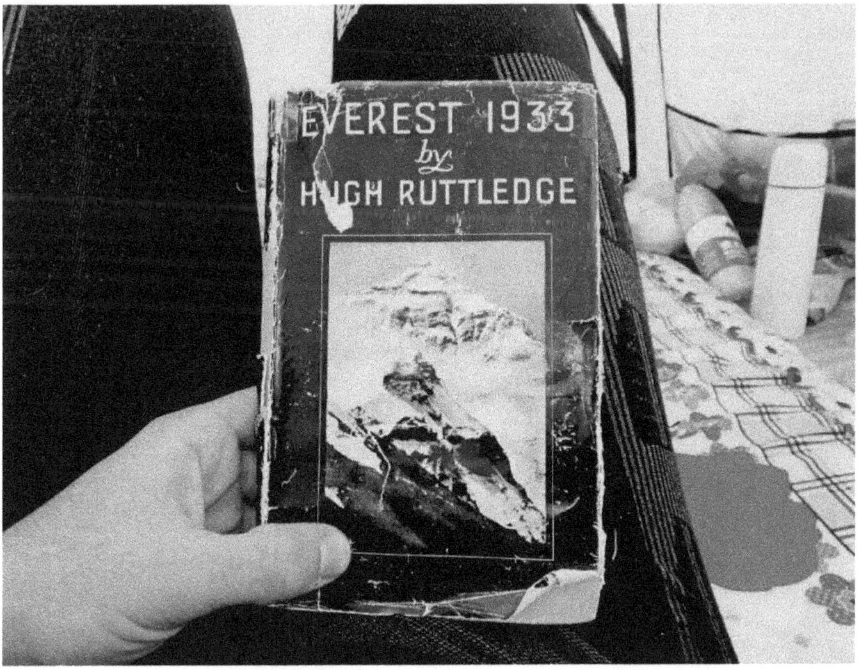

The book about Everest with Mallory

The trek above Base Camp

On May 17, after breakfast, it was announced once again that there were no signs of an improvement in the weather and the Chinese would go back to work on the guide rope. The forecast was that there would be no ascent before May 28. I was getting very tired of the tension between the members of our camp and the constant boredom. The chief officer of the Base Camp with whom I had travelled to Zangmu, and I had become good friends. He invited me to go down with him to Tingri for two days. He didn't want any money from me, because I had already paid twice, and the third time it would be free. My heart jumped with joy. I really wanted to go down, especially because I wanted to soak again in that mineral water near Tingri before the final ascent.

It took me exactly five minutes to pack my rucksack, and I was in the jeep with my friends the driver and the officer. The road to Tingri is about 90 km and takes about three or four hours, depending on the driver and the car. It can take up to six hours. When we were halfway, Mingma (our Serdar) called the officer to tell me that there was a new weather forecast, and a window was expected on May 24 and 25. He told me to go back to the camp because the next day (May 18) all the members were going to the next camp towards the top. At first I wasn't sure about going back, I really wanted to go the mineral baths. More importantly the others were planning to leave on May 18 to spend two nights at the Front Base Camp at 6,440 metres. I had already discovered that I was unable to recover at that height, and I had decided that for my final ascent I would only stay only one night on ABC before heading up. So I decided to continue on my way to the mineral baths and instead of two nights, stay in Tingri for just one. Then I would return on May 18 to Base Camp and on May 19 to go up to the Roof of the World.

In Tingri we just stopped to eat at an inn and continued to the pool, about 25 kilometres from the city, in the direction of Nyalam. The officer and the driver also wanted to bathe in the mineral water, but they weren't going to sleep here, but in Tingri, where they didn't have to pay at the hotel. However, I decided to sleep in the motel next to the mineral water. There were several rooms and the prices were very affordable. They included breakfast and dinner. I took a room for one night and immediately jumped into the pool. The officer and the driver were already relaxing in the outdoor pool. I put the plug in the inner pool to fill it with water.

The outdoor pool is formed from a natural rock bed with hot water springs, which you can't mix with cold. The water is really murky, full of algae and all manner of other things swimming in it. Who cares, you're at 4400 metres above sea level and enjoying soaking in a natural mineral pool with a view of Everest and Cho Oyu? What more does a person need? The others ordered beer and offered me one as well, but I was still as shy when it came to alcohol, so I stuck to water. I didn't want to risk getting a sore throat, because the air temperature was no more than 3-4 degrees and there was a strong wind. After about an hour in the outdoor pool, I said goodbye to my friends. We agreed they would pick me up the next day, after breakfast at 10.30, to return to Base Camp. After the outdoor pool, I moved to the indoor pool which had already filled with water and it was out of the wind. The polycarbonate roof was broken and the wind was blowing through it. There was a crack in the bottom of the inner pool between the rocks where the water came in. It was more pleasant here. I could shave and wash in peace. The others had shaved and washed in the outdoor pool, and all manner of other things were done there. Even the fruits and vegetables for the restaurant were washed there. If you're too squeamish, you'll end up hungry, thirsty and cold. There are no bathrooms or water in the rooms. I shaved in the indoor pool. I didn't want to meet the Goddess with a beard, and then washed my clothes so that they would be clean for the final ascent. I took care not to overdo it with the mineral water and put too much strain on my heart, and not be able to sleep.

After the spa treatments, I returned to my room and found that the temperature was a whole five degrees. That was hot for here. I dressed at lightning speed and put on all the clothes I had, and cuddled up in bed with whatever I could find. They seemed to have a tradition of not changing the sheets after each client, perhaps only once a month. There was nothing I could do about that. I just got into bed. I was wearing three pairs of trousers and five layers of clothing. I had no direct contact with their bed linen, and the electricity couldn't cope with the cold anyway.

My room overlooked the Goddess and Cho Oyu. The window frames were more suitable for a pigsty or a cowshed and they let in a strong draft. However, I stuffed the curtains into the gaps to seal the windows a little and stop the wind blowing me away. I rested in bed for about an hour and then as hungry as a wolf I went down to the inn. There were a lot of Tibetans there. It was Saturday and full of guests, but I had no idea what would happen that night. I ordered rice with vegetables and vegetable soup. The food was delicious everywhere and I really liked their cuisine. There was no hygiene, no running water in the restaurant, but I didn't have any stomach problems, as I often did after visiting most restaurants in Bulgaria. I had a delicious meal and enjoyed life with the friendly Tibetan people. From time to time someone would come and sit with me, to try and chat. They tried to sell things to me.

They were good-natured people struggling to survive. Unfortunately they seemed to have forgotten many of their priceless traditions. Gradually the restaurant filled up. Outside more and more people began to arrive in groups to bathe in the pools. It was already dark and I didn't expect the pool to be full of people all night until the morning. Inside the restaurant, there were men gambling at every table. It was like being in a casino. Dice, checkers, cards and all manner of games, every gambler hoping to win something. Judging by the money in front of everyone, they were betting quite a lot, somewhere in the range of 50-100 Euro per game. It was no joke. I was sure that is was the system here that had turned them into gamblers who liked nothing more than to eat, drink and smoke, looking for entertainment and easy money. Not that the rest of the world is any different in that regard. From what I had read over the years about Tibet and their culture, there seemed sadly to be nothing left of it but salaried monks in the monasteries as a tourist attraction. You could say the same about most of the monasteries in Bulgaria. They've forgotten about the spiritual side of things, and are more interested in the material, and entertainment.

I felt sorry for these people who were so intent on gambling, each with a cigarette in their mouth. The Tibetans smoke very heavily. When I came to Tibet four years previously, I had had no contact with the local people as I did on this expedition, and I wasn't aware of the reality. As sad as I was, I couldn't have changed anything, and did I really need to? It's true they didn't have much choice and weren't able to live where they chose, like us. Leaving the country, even on an excursion, is very difficult. They don't even have passports.

The evening was great fun, as the only white man with my long hair, I was the centre of attraction. The children came to play with me. There was a party all night in the outside pool. Most of the men and women didn't have bathing costumes and were packed in like sardines next to each other. They were clearly more progressive than us in this respect. I've been to plenty of water parks in Germany which after a certain time at the weekend turn into nudist pools and hundreds of people bathe and walk around them completely naked. Outside the temperatures were well below zero, but everyone was bathing and having fun. I forgot to mention that in the restaurant, apart from the high stakes gambling, there was a lot of drinking going on as well. You have no idea what quantity of alcohol was drunk. They weren't ordering by the can, but by twelve packs. Next to each table there were packs and boxes of beer. New ones were constantly being brought out. They were all downing beer, while some others were drinking spirits from small glasses washed down with beer. It wasn't a pretty picture, but the important thing was that they felt good and were having fun. I don't know what they did during the week, and what sort of work they did, but they were definitely above the average economic level for Tibetans in Tibet province, China. They all had cars parked out in front, some were even brand new. I took some pictures of the piles of empty beer cans and money on the tables, being careful not to hurt anyone. That evening they must have got through 10-20 beers each. What was most interesting was that the women drank just as much. The men and women didn't sit at the same table, there was a strict allocation of places and everyone knew their place. The women also gamble, but with smaller stakes and drank liqueur. At about 23.00, I decided to go to bed, because I needed to conserve my strength for tomorrow. But it was so noisy. The rooms on either side were occupied and there was gambling and drinking in industrial quantities going on. I had forgotten my earplugs and I couldn't sleep. It was dawn before I finally managed to get some sleep, for two or three hours at most. But I wasn't tired. I was excited that I would be going to the top tomorrow.

These bars saved my life, thanks to Yavor and ImBio

I was made doughnuts with jam for breakfast. There were sacks full of beer cans outside. Everything was clean and tidy, as if there had been no party in there all night. Just as I was having breakfast, the officer arrived in the Landcruiser and we headed back to Tingri. However, to my great surprise, instead of taking the road to Base Camp from the centre of Tingri, we continued on and a few kilometres after Tingri we turned south, to Base Camp, but on a completely different road, unknown to me. That was when they told me that we would be picking up a Russian from Seven Summits who was resting in a town about 40 km east of Base Camp. I was in no hurry. I didn't really have anything to do at Base Camp? My luggage was already packed to move out the next day.

We were travelling along a dirt road which was much worse, passing through a number of villages on the way. We entered a beautiful valley through a series of little hamlets and villages. It was about 400 metres lower and for the first time I saw big trees, green leaves and vegetation. It was like a beautiful, green oasis. In a number of places the Liberators, as the Chinese are referred to in Tibet, were building big bridges and a big new road. I imagined it wouldn't be too long before this road would be asphalted too, like the road to Everest where there are already plans to build a modern base hotel with all the extras like oxygen rooms. The time will come.

We travelled for a number of hours, having to drive very slowly in certain places. I don't know how many kilometres we drove, but it was afternoon before we arrived in a town situated in the lowest spot in the region where the rivers meet. We had descended to below 4000 metres and the vegetation was quite lush. We had a lovely meal at the local restaurant, and as always the officer ordered spicy and delicious vegetable dishes. When we had eaten, the Russian whom we were due to take to Base Camp appeared. He had paid for this entire detour. He paid them $300 to take him back to Base Camp so he could get a start tomorrow, like me.

We set off for Base Camp and the car started causing problems again, even though it had just been repaired. It was just too many kilometres for it, along dirt roads rather than asphalt. I sat with the Russian in the back, chatting. He told me about himself and I told him about myself. He lived with his wife and three children in China, in a big city on the ocean. He was paid really well, but he didn't want to stay in

China. He wanted to move somewhere else. The children already spoke Mandarin, but he didn't understand a word. We passed through another couple of villages until we joined the road from Tingri. We arrived at the Base Camp at about 6 p.m. We had spent all day on the road, but it had been interesting to see new lands and areas. The only person left here was David. Like me, he had decided to sleep only one night at 6440 metres and head out a day after the others.

There were only three of us at dinner — me, David, and his girlfriend — I think her name was Adina. Nothing in particular happened, we all and went back to our tents. I couldn't get to sleep. I was too excited that the day was coming when I would be heading for the top again. I like going to the tops of mountains. I feel my life and live it the way I understand it.

THE ASCENT TO THE TOP, OR FROM BASE CAMP TO THE SUMMIT OF CHOMOLUNGMA, 8848 METRES AND BACK TO BASE CAMP

From day 45 to day 52

Setting off in the direction of the summit from Base Camp, 5200 metres

DAY 45

May 19, 2014

CHINESE BASE CAMP, 5200 metres

I slept fitfully, the wind was very strong, buffeting the tent. It was also very windy in the morning, but the decision had been made. After breakfast, I would be heading out for the Intermediate Camp at 5800 metres. I wondered whether I shouldn't stay one more day at the Base Camp and then head directly to the Advance Base Camp, without sleeping at the Intermediate Camp. However, I thought there was no point in overloading myself unnecessarily. After breakfast I packed my rucksack and for the fourth time I headed towards the Intermediate Camp. It was the seventh time I had walked this route and I already knew every stone, I thought that I could do it even in the snow. What I didn't know was that it was very difficult to walk if there are no yaks in front of you to feel for the road.

Light snow had begun to fall and there was a strong wind blowing. I dressed well, took the sleeping bag I used at Base Camp and which I always took to Intermediate Camp and then returned to Base Camp. There were other expeditions heading up the mountain today. There were also yaks along the way. The only thing I could think of was the top and when would the Goddess promise me good weather. I walked slowly, there was no need to hurry, and the wind was very strong. On the way up, I bumped into the Russian I had met the day before in the car for Base Camp. The Seven Summits Club had split into two groups because there were too many people for everyone to sleep together in camps 1, 2 and 3. Both groups would be using the same tents. The first group had left the day before, and today it was the turn of the second. The idea was for those who left on May 18 to reach the top on May 24, while those who left on May 19 to reach it on May 25. There are five more camps from the Base Camp to the summit. That means a minimum of six days if you only stay one night at each camp.

So, I headed out on May 19, but planned to climb to the top on May

24. I didn't want to spend two nights at the Advance Base Camp at 6,440 metres like 90 percent of the expedition climbers.

As always I walked alone on this 20-kilometre section between Base and Intermediate Camp. The strong wind didn't abate and with only a single break, it took me about five hours to reach our Intermediate Camp. The camp manager who had been here for more than a month without descending didn't look at all well. He complained to me that he felt very ill, especially psychologically and couldn't sleep at all. They had just been waiting for David and me to sleep here, and then next day they would strike the Intermediate Camp and take everything back down to the Base Camp. The season was almost over for this year. There was nothing left to eat. He just boiled me some water, I had my own soup and poured hot water over it.

Rest stop between Base and Intermediate Camp

With the youngest woman in the world ever to climb Everest - next to me, and her three guides from India, 5,800 metres.

A little later three boys and a girl from India came. They were with another company, but they didn't have a camp here, they had come to eat and sleep in ours. Then I realized that at 14 years of age, the girl was the youngest climber in the world, trying to set a new record. In addition to the Sherpas, she had these three young boys to help her. She looked at least 17 years old, in very good physical condition and mental health. They had their own cook who carried their own food and quickly cooked their own dishes. Of course, they invited me to eat with them. The dishes were delicious but with different spices, especially if you compare them with those of our chefs. I spoke to the Indians, they all spoke English, one of them even better than me. We filled our thermos flasks with hot water for the night and we all went back to our own tents. The Indians would also be sleeping two nights at the Advance Base and then head up.

DAY 46

May 20, 2014

I had a good night in my warm sleeping bag. As usual, the temperatures in the tent only fell to about minus 12-13 degrees and it was pleasantly cold. I got up two or three times to fill my bottles and fell asleep again. I was still drinking water at night for better acclimatization, even though I was already feeling like I was at sea level. There was no difference in my pulse, in my walking, or in my strength.

I got up early in the morning. A couple of centimetres of fresh snow had fallen obscuring the path. My tent was two metres from the path that everyone used. I ate with the Indians again. They had cooked something like pancakes, and they even brought their own jam and treated everyone. I imagine it was to return the favour for sleeping in my company's tents...

After breakfast, I packed my rucksack. I left my sleeping bag with the Tibetan and using plenty of gestures, facial expressions and signs I explained to him that I didn't want him sleeping in my bag or smoking cigarettes in it for the next couple of days until they broke camp and went back down to Base Camp. He seemed to understand me. Not that it mattered any more. My real sleeping bag, the one I would get to the top with, was waiting for me in the Advance Camp. I headed out alone again.

There were some Russians in front of me, the same ones I had overtaken in the beginning. I walked quite quickly, focused on the path which had changed because of the higher temperatures and the ensuing storm. The path had changed in places and I had to cross new rivers. However, the main path was the same and I made quite rapid progress. I took a break at the place where I always stopped - at the yakmen's tent. This time, however, the tent was no longer there. It too had been taken down. The wind was still blowing hard, with no sign that it would stop soon. The forecast was for bad weather until the evening of May 23, improving only on the morning of May 24. But it was still only a forecast and nothing was certain.

When I reached the place where I had fallen into the water the previous time, I decided not to cross there but went around the whole lake. The views were beautiful and inspiring despite the strong wind. About one o'clock in the afternoon I was at the ABC, just in time for lunch. Everyone on my expedition had been here since the day before. Today would be their second night, and the next day we would all head on up together. The Advance Base Camp was bigger than I had ever seen it. A lot of new companies had joined with their own tents. They must have acclimatised elsewhere and only came for the final ascent of Everest. It was like a village gathering. As soon as I arrived, I was told that it wasn't certain if the weather would be suitable on May 24, and the guide rope hadn't been installed to the top. The forecast wasn't good. To be safe, my Sherpa Gilgen wanted us to go to Camp 1 on May 22, and then make our final ascent if possible on the 25th May.

The wind at the Advance Base Camp was very strong too, and it was impossible to stay outside for long. After lunch, everyone went back to their tents and wondered what to do. I decided to leave it to the morning before I made my decision, but I was more inclined to head out the next day. I liked the idea of getting to the top on the 24th May. Even back in Bulgaria before I came, I thought about getting to the top on the 24th, the Bulgarian national day. Even though it's completely impossible to predict when there will be a window.

The evening was spent discussing all kinds of programs and strategies. There weren't many options. You either go to Camp 1 on the 21st or you stay another day and wait. Most of them preferred to stay a third night in the camp. The only one who wanted to ascend was Richard because he had a schedule to get to Denali and he would miss his flight. Bill was also leaving the next day. His plan was to spend two days at Camp 3 at 8,300 metres with his two Sherpas and twelve bottles of oxygen. He would rest there before his final ascent on the summit on May 25.

In front of Advance Base Camp, 6200 metres

DAY 47

May 21 2014

There was a strong wind during the night and it snowed a little. I slept well and felt in great shape. When breakfast time came, everyone was still wondering what to do. Bill was the only one sure that he would going up. I said I would be going up as well. At first my Sherpa objected. He wanted us to stay for another day, but he finally agreed and as windy and unsuitable as it was to head for Camp 1, after breakfast we packed our bags and left. We were followed by the two Poles, Kristiano and Richard with their Sherpas, and David with his Sherpa. The only ones to remain were the two Indians. They wanted to spend a third consecutive night at the Advance Camp, to be certain that the guide rope would be completed by May 25.

Gilgen hung back a bit at the camp, and we agreed to meet at the place for crampons and seats. When I arrived, Grandpa Bill was already being helped by his two Sherpas to put on his seat and crampons. He was already wearing his oxygen mask, and breathing life saving gas. After a while, my Sherpa arrived. We weren't in any hurry. Whatever happened we would get to Camp 1 today. After fitting ourselves out, we went over the glacier to the base of the wall. This would be the third time I had climbed the wall during this expedition. The first time wearing my Batura climbing boots it had been easier, but the second time with my Olympus boots it was much harder.

We walked slowly, each with his own thoughts in his head. The wind was very strong, and in a couple of places I fell through the ice. Out of force of habit, I left one stick at the base of the wall. I already knew the advantage of holding the Jumara ascender in one hand and using the other to pull up with the stick. Most people, and a lot of climbers especially, have little idea of the benefits of using a stick, even when climbing walls. The first part of the ascent at the base was almost vertical. It had deteriorated even more after a whole month of climbing and it took a long time to pass. We were followed by a large group of over twenty Chinese (Tibetans) from their mountain service. They were due to reach Camp 3 the next day and install the guide rope from 8,300 metres to the top on the 23rd of May. They had no other choice, they had come to earn some money for their family and to feed their children.

I noticed that most of the young lads had photographs of their families, wives, and their children on the shoulders of their down-filled suits in place of their sponsors' logos. It was so sad and touching that each of them knew he might not come back alive from here. We were all very aware of that. Every second where we were now, in the middle of the North Cole wall, an avalanche could form, a crack could open, or even the whole mountain could collapse on us, and neither the guide rope nor any other technical device could help us. Many people died right here. Two or three years ago on the same route, David's partner had fallen through a fissure when descending from acclimatization at Camp 1. David had been walking in front and his partner about 20-30 metres behind him. David said that at one point he had turned around and his partner wasn't there. He returned to look for him, but only found a large fissure and his partner had disappeared. Never to be seen again. Right here on North Col.

We had to take a lot of rests. The going was difficult for the Sherpa and me. Were we tired and running out of time, whether it was the bad weather conditions, or an energy saving mechanism had come into play, but we tried to move on up using minimal amounts of energy. The weather was bad, snow, wind, cold, fog ... It was a good job that there was no one descending in the opposite direction. There was no room to pass, especially in the narrowest sections where there was barely enough room for one.

I don't know exactly how many hours it took us to get to Camp 1, but it was definitely the longest and most difficult of my three climbs. The tent was covered in snow, but at least it was there. During the last two weeks of the storm, a number of tents had been blown away from Camp 1. Those like David who pitched tents at Camp 2, returned to find nothing. There was no sign of the tents. It was very cold at Camp 1 at 7100 metres. I was tired, but best of all I was hungry and thirsty. That was a good sign that I was well and healthy. We made our way to the tent and cleared it. Inside were the inflatable covering and a down-filled suit I had left on May 7 so I wouldn't have to carry them up the wall again. I was a little concerned that my suit would be all right after two weeks of blizzards and storms, but there it was waiting for me.

There was heavy snow falling on Camp 1. It was piling up. We went to the shared tent where most of the Sherpas had gathered, and melted drinking water for cooking. I filled my thermos with water and retired to our tent. My watch showed minus 12 degrees Celsius, and it was still bright outside. How much colder would it get?

Gilgen brought some boiling water and poured it over a packet of spaghetti with vegetables. I don't know what he ate with the other Sherpas in their common tent. Late in the evening, Bill and the two Poles arrived. I don't know when David arrived. The weather forecast wasn't good at all. There was no news whether the Chinese had reached

Camp 3 to install the guide rope for the next day. Everyone started wondering and grumbling about what we were going to do. But there was only one way for me and it was up. I couldn't sleep that evening, I just lay waiting for the time to pass. You think about all sorts of things, you dream, you wonder ... You can't sleep a wink, whether because of the altitude or the excitement about what will happen the next day. The next day every metre above 7250 would be the highest altitude I had climbed in my life. Every metre above 7250 would be a personal record.

I had spaghetti for dinner in the tent at Camp 1, North Col, 7,100 metres, North Ridge of Everest.

DAY 48

May 22 2014

I don't know if I dosed even a little that night. I was constantly watching the time and temperature. Not that it was that important, but I did it to break the boredom. It was minus 16 in the morning, but I was comfortable in my sleeping bag. I was just wondering where all this oxygen was coming from, I was breathing well. My Gilgen was resilient and was lying there in his sleeping bag, his mouth poking out and breathing as if he was in his village at 4400 metres above sea level. I couldn't let myself breathe the cold air. I had to be careful, especially knowing how susceptible I was to the cold. It was all thanks to my stable psyche that I was safe and sound. I know that there are no impossible things and if I really want something, I make sure I achieve it.

I don't remember what time we got up in the morning, the wind had calmed down a bit. There was a large gas stove and a melting pot in the common tent. We melted some snow, I poured hot water over the muesli and had breakfast. Eventually the others emerged and the panic began - not only in our camp but in all the other camps that were here. The question was whether to head up or not. They were told by radio that no one had yet reached Camp 3. That meant that the guide rope hadn't yet been installed and the weather in Camp 2 was very cold. We spent another two hours wondering what to do, and I was all set to go up. Other than us, there weren't many people there, just the five members and the six Sherpas. There seven or eight Russians, each with his own Sherpa and guide. I think there were two other Poles and two Frenchmen. I didn't see anyone from Kobler at the ABC that day, but there may have been. Bill was going up anyway, because, as I said, he had enough oxygen to stay in Camp 3 and he didn't care too much anyway.

After much debate, the decision was made that who wanted to go on up, should go, and who wanted to stay, should stay. Gilgen and I, of course, decided to head on up. The climb up to Camp 2 was beautiful and the wind was blowing hard. The wind was so strong that I could barely stand in certain places but I was attached to the guide rope and kept moving up. My Sherpa and I were amongst the last to head out to Camp 2, but in our own style we son started overtaking them. By this time I had a bottle of oxygen in my backpack, and so did my Sherpa. If it hadn't been for the wind, the climb up the Northern face would have been wonderful. I wouldn't say that it was extremely hard going or difficult. There's an incline, but it's nothing special and quite easy to walk. We stopped a few times to rest, and I turned back to admire the landscape and the peaks around us. The views were marvellous. So beautiful.

About midway, we stopped to eat and decided to put on our oxygen masks. It must have been about 7500 metres. I wasn't having a problem breathing normally. I was out of breath, but I get out breath in Bulgaria when I have to carry a heavy rucksack up a steep slope. We had the bottles with us anyway, so we decided that we may as well breathe oxygen. The oxygen mask is connected to the regulator which is attached to the bottle. The regulator of the bottle has 4 settings, as well as a half setting at 0.5. It regulates the amount of oxygen you take in. The higher the number from 0 to 4, the more oxygen you get, but the faster your bottle runs out. We turned to regulators to one. We weren't at a great altitude yet, so it wasn't too difficult. Some time at around 4 pm we reached Camp 2 at 7700 metres. Camp is perhaps to use too strong a word. It was about 600-700 metres long and at least 100 metres difference in altitude from one end to other, along steep and tooth-sharp rocks. You have to climb over them and look for a suitable place to pitch your tent. There were many torn tents and tent poles here.

Camp 2, 7700 m, Northern edge of Everest

Our tent at Camp 2, 7700 metres

We kept on going up looking for a place. I had the feeling that the wind was getting stronger the higher we went up. We barely found 5-6 square metres just enough to pitch our tent to the left of the path, on a large slope. There had been a tent here, and there were some poles and torn pieces of a tent. It was on the very edge of the North face and the wind was freezing and incredibly strong. We decided to pitch it there. It was a good thing that Gilgen had experience in pitching a tent in a very strong wind. First after we took it out of the bag, we tied both ends to some rocks. Gilgen used some old guide rope to tie the tent. Then I held one end of it, and he threaded the tent poles. When we tried to straighten it. I had never seen anything like it. The tent was tied to the rocks in two places, like an animal brought to slaughter. I held tightly on to a third rope while the wind wanted to blow the tent away... and us with it. It was a big fight. With supreme effort we managed to raise the tent and make it fast. And all this in just a couple of square metres, with a precipice on one side. We followed this by trying to put the cover over the tent. This also required a lot of time and effort in this relentless hurricane wind. The last operation was the most important.

We needed to secure the tent fast, so that we didn't fall into the along with it. We cut some ropes from the old guide ropes to the top and tied the tent to nearby rocks and stones. After about half an hour of a life and death struggle with the wind, the tent was ready for us to move into. We needed to be alert all the time.

But the views? The views you could only see from Camp 2! I took photographs and some video recordings as well. We removed our masks from time to time to talk. When you remove the mask, for the first 10-15 minutes you don't feel that you're so high or that the oxygen content is so low.

Spaghetti for dinner again! There was nothing remarkable about that evening. The winds buffeted us as if they were chasing in each other in a race. We were inside the tent meditating. I needed to go to the toilet. But with these overalls and the wind outside. It was a big problem. There was nothing I could do about it, I had to go out. Gilgen just yelled at me to grab the guide rope, so I wasn't blown away by the wind. It wasn't funny. And because you can't relieve yourself directly on the path, you have to move a little to the left above the precipice and you're holding on to some old guide ropes. Enough excitement to last me a lifetime. I managed to do what I had to do with a certain dignity and returned to the tent alive and well. I never imagined that such strong winds existed. I had the feeling that the tent was about to take off any moment. The wind was blowing so hard and buffeting against the tent, that we could barely hear what we were talking about.

In the tent at Camp 2, 7700 metres, North edge

DAY 49

May 23 2014

All night the wind blew so hard that I had no idea how the tent didn't take off. It was a real miracle. I didn't get a wink of sleep. The regulator was at 0.5. This is 0.5 litres of oxygen per minute, 30 litres per hour. A single bottle contains four litres of compressed oxygen at 200 atmospheres. That makes 800 litres, sufficient for about 28 hours at setting 0.5; 14 hours at 1; seven hours at 2; or 3.5 hours at 4. Russian regulators had 6 settings, and their members had 7 bottles per person. I had three bottles, and so did my Sherpa.

In the morning we waited for the sun to rise and warm the tent a little inside despite the strong wind. We had no appetite. We shared a small packet of spaghetti again which is basically enough for one person. We ate a little and melted ice for water. We filled our thermoses and began to get ready to head out earlier rather than later, since the wind grew stronger as the day progressed. We also had to pack the tent for the next camp. Packing it was faster than pitching it and by around 9.30 we were ready to start for Camp 3. As for the other members of our expedition, I had no idea who slept where. It was a fight for survival, and there's no time and opportunity for other things.

On May 23, we were the first to go to the next camp and no one overtook us. The wind was very strong that day too with no prospect of calming down. We walked up the mountain along a path of snow, ice, rocks and boulders. From time to time we stopped to rest and admire the amazing views. Above 8,000 metres the sky was different, I could feel the altitude despite the mask. It wasn't the thin air, but something different. There were crows flying higher than us. These birds were clearly not affected by the low useful oxygen content at these altitudes. In some places it was quite steep and we had to climb with both hands. Gilgen made me leave my stick in Camp 2. He said I wouldn't need to climb this section and I needed both hands free. I did what he told me, although I was beginning to regret it. I would recommend having a stick in your rucksack on the way to the top. If you don't need it, you keep it attached to your pack. It weighs nothing, but is so useful. So, from Camp 2 onwards, I only had my legs to rely on.

Between Camp 2 and Camp 3, about 8,000 metres, North Ridge.

Between Camp 2 and Camp 3 at about 8100 metres. Changtse Peak, 7550 metres, behind me.

The wind continued to blow hard until we crossed to the other side of the North Edge, on the right, in the sheltered side of Everest. The wind was blowing from the west, and we were on the east side of the mountain. Now suddenly it was as if the wind had dropped considerably. That was very, very nice. We took a rest. We also met some Chinese climbers from the mountain service on their way down. They assured us that their group had gone all the way to install the missing guide rope to the summit. That was already good news.

We had another steep climb ahead of us on mixed terrain between rocks and ice. By about 14.00 hrs we reached Camp 3 at 8300 metres. The wind had abated and the top was within arm's reach. I could see the route we would be taking that evening. There was a channel and then the path continues to the right. There weren't many tents in the camp. Just a few used by the group who had installed the guide rope. But there were plenty of torn tents and poles left over from other climbers. There were birds circling above us. I could only imagine what they were looking for here and what they found to eat. We didn't waste much food for them to feed on. We were the first to arrive at the Camp. We chose a flat spot where there had been a tent, of which only fragments remained. This time the tent was much easier to pitch and tie down. We collected some ice and started melting it. It seemed to take an eternity for the ice to melt. It took maybe more than an hour to get the water we needed. There was a nice afternoon sun and it was pleasantly warm in the tent. I took my mask off from time to time and breathed calmly. It didn't feel like I was at 8300 metres. I imagine that was because a sufficient number of red blood cells had formed in my blood. Over a space of 10-20 minutes without a mask, I didn't feel any difference, and I wasn't performing any physical action. I eventually I put on my second oxygen bottle. In the tent we also kept the regulator valve set at 0.5. It got so hot in the sun that I even stripped down to my thermal underwear. That evening the group that had installed the guide ropes came down. They told us that everything was ready, all the way to the top and we could head on up when we wanted to. There were things I needed to do in the tent, my socks were wet and I had to dry them, as well as my triple- layered boots. I took a few photographs and a little bit of video. I tried not to use my camera or video recorder too much. I wanted to save the batteries for the top.

It had been a week since I had last talked to anyone from Bulgaria on the satellite phone. So no one had any idea where I was or that tonight would be my final assault on the summit. I didn't want my mother and father to be worried. I had decided to call them after I had reached the top and was back in Camp 3. Then I would tell them that everything was fine and that I was on my way down. I had no intention of carrying the satellite phone to the top ... There wasn't any point. If anything happened to you, God forbid, above Camp 3, there was no-one who could come to your rescue. I could rely only on myself and to a certain extent on my partner Gilgen. And he would be fighting for his own life tonight.

Gilgen and I chatted and rested in the tent. After about two or three hours, perhaps more, the two Poles arrived with their Sherpas. Then David arrived with his Sherpa who was the record holder for climbs in our expedition, and then finally Bill with his two assistants. Bill was now 72 years old. In 2009 he had climbed to the top from Nepal, making him the oldest American to conquer Everest. Since then, every year he has attempted to reach the summit of Everest from the Tibetan side. On occasions he reached Step 2 at about 8,600 metres before descending. This year, however, he had a new strategy.

We were all pitched close to each other, and the Russians just above us. The Russians, besides having one or two Sherpas, also had guides for every three clients. In our expedition, Richard was Kristiano's guide and the Ukrainian Victor was Alexander's. However, Victor was no longer with us because the oligarch, Alexander, had given up.

As Gilgen and I were lying in our tent, Kristiano's Sherpa came in and said that there was no room for him in their tent, and would we let him into ours. What? The two Poles and their Sherpas had only one tent. Kristiano, Richard, and Richard's Sherpa would be in their only tent, while this Sherpa Minjo would be with us. I wasn't happy with their tricks. Why should we two drag everything up with us, while these other four bring up only a single tent? A really dirty trick. I don't know if this had been arranged with Gilgen in advance or not, but there wasn't enough room. The next few hours before heading on up were quite uncomfortable. Bill and his two Sherpas were also in a single tent, while David and his Sherpa were alone.

At about 18.00 David was getting itchy feet and decided to attempt the summit. He was barely able to stand on his feet, and it would be an absolute miracle if he reached the top in that condition. We had decided to leave at 20.30. Each team made up their own mind when to leave and what route to take. No one was dependent on anyone else. Gilgen and I rested in the tent. In the evening we shared another packet of spaghetti with vegetables. I had some nuts in my pockets and some vegan bars that I gave to Gilgen. He liked them very much. I was neither hungry, nor cold, nor thirsty or tired. I had made my mind up to reach the top at sunrise, according to my old custom.

Three of us in the tent before we go to the top.

At 19:00 Nepal time we started our preparations. I'd brought also my sleeping bag with me, but I didn't even take it out of its bag. While it was warm, I had taken off my overalls, then I put it back on again for the departure. When the evening came I was fully dressed in my down-filled suit and boots. No one could predict what would happen, so I had to bring it with me to Camp 3. David had told me that he too would be bringing a sleeping bag to Camp 3 and would stay in his down-filled clothes. That way he wouldn't have to carry another two or three kilograms of luggage. That's actually a good idea for future expeditions because you only have a few hours rest in Camp 3 before the assault on the summit. It was difficult for three big men to get dressed in the tent, attach the seats, adjust head torches and equipment. There was water to be melted, of course, and other things which needed to be done. Everything took considerably longer than at lower altitudes.

We had planned to move out at 20.30. By now it was 21.00 and at around 21.15 we went up. A lot of head torches could be seen ahead of us. Right away we overtook Richard and Kristiano. Gradually we caught up with the Russians, whom we also overtook. We were walking at an incredible pace. I led and Gilgen followed. The wind was light. I wasn't feeling cold, and the temperature was probably about minus 20-23 degrees. It wasn't long before we caught up with David and his Sherpa, who had left first.

David was in poor health and could neither speak nor walk. The man was fighting hard. The terrain was rocky, ice and snow. We initially walked along the channel, then alternating steep and flat sections. The steep sections required that you climbed with both hands and feet, while using the Jumara ascender to pull yourself up.

A light snow had begun to fall with a light wind. The altitude was about 8450 metres above sea level. My watch was showing 23.00, Nepalese time, it had been about an hour and a half since my Sherpa and I had left Camp 3 at 8,300 metres. Although we had been the last to leave that evening, we were now ahead of all the others and we had been leading for some time. It had snowed softly during the day and there was about four inches of fresh snow. I was in the lead and the Sherpa followed me about two or three metres behind. Earlier in the day, the men from the Chinese Tibetan Mountaineering Organization had set up a guide rope to the peak. They had had to wait for two weeks until the weather was suitable, but they were clearly in a hurry there was only about a hundred or so metres or guide rope. The visibility was poor, only as far as the head torch. We kept tightly to the guide rope to which we were attached by the Jumara ascender. When we had to, we used it to pull ourselves up. Some places were very steep and we had to climb on our hands and feet over the snow-covered rocks. About 20 minutes after the light snow began to fall, we reached a very steep passage at an altitude of about 8500 metres.

I am ready for the final march to the top.

It was then that the Sherpa shouted to me that the weather was getting worse and we wouldn't be able to reach the top today. He said we had to go back. The snowflakes were very small and the wind was very light. According to the forecast the weather was supposed to get better after midnight. I objected and told him that I thought the weather at the moment wasn't too bad, and there was no point in standing still or going down. I told him that I thought we should keep going. We had stopped in an extremely uncomfortable place. With one hand I was holding on to the Jumara while standing on one leg. It was very steep and I had to constantly shift the weight of my body from one leg to the other.

The Sherpa radioed the expedition Serdar at Advance Base Camp (ABC) at 6,400 metres, and told him that the weather was getting worse, and we would have to go down. I also spoke to the Serdar, who told me that the other two members of our expedition, Kristiano and Richard from Poland, were already descending. I was very surprised because Richard was a professional climbing Everest for the fifth time with his client. At the time, I didn't yet know the real reason for their decision to give up. After about half an hour of discussion standing on one leg and hanging on to the guide rope, the Sherpa and I walked back down to Camp 3. I knew very well that there wouldn't be a second chance, since I had started using up my oxygen kind of and I wouldn't have enough for a second attempt on the top the next day. Everything inside me was crying out that the weather wasn't that bad and I wanted to carry on up to the top. I felt extremely strong and in good shape. I felt neither cold nor fear and had no doubt that I would reach the top. We were so far ahead of the others who had set out before us that none of them had caught up, even though we had been standing still for so long. I went down past my Sherpa and wondered what to do. It made no sense to descend just because of the light snow. I knew that the Sherpas were unreliable, especially above 8,300 metres. I had even heard of many cases of climbers abandoned by their Sherpas.

After about 10-15 minutes we reached David from Hungary and his Sherpa, from my expedition. It was David's seventh attempt in a row to reach the peak without using artificial oxygen, only with the help of his Sherpa. He had left Camp 3 three hours before us and was having a hard time moving. He looked wretched, exhausted, without a gram of strength left. However, he wasn't going back. I couldn't believe how hard he was fighting. We stayed with them and talked about the weather. David was in terrible shape, kneeling in the snow and breathing very hard. We took some photographs, or rather the Sherpas took pictures of us as proof that we had reached 8300 metres, so that they could get their full pay for getting us to the peak. I was still reluctant to go down. At that moment, at about ten metres away from us, my Sherpa shone his headlight on the corpse of a climber lying on his stomach upside down and arms outstretched. He may have been there for several years. The Sherpa proudly asked me if I wanted to remain there like that dead man. It was an absurd comparison since it was only because of Gilgen that we had been standing in one place for the past hour, me on one leg, and that he was even suggesting going down. The temperature was well below zero, and only my down-filled clothes kept me from freezing. There was another long discussion and phone call, and we started on down again. By now we had lost about 100 metres of altitude and about an hour after our first stop.

Then I saw the leaders of the next group moving towards us. So I stopped and told the Sherpa that I wasn't going down. I asked him to give me the oxygen bottle he was carrying for me so that I could go up on my own. No one could stop me now. I had made the decision and there was not to be no more discussion. He was quite taken aback and radioed the Serdar again. After his radio conversation, he told me that the Serdar had received a new weather forecast, which was more favourable and that we could proceed safely to the top. By now a group of Russians with their Sherpas had already caught up with us. We started the ascent again. I led the column of about seven Russians, a Pole and the corresponding number of Sherpas. Tears of excitement welled up in my eyes ... I was walking in the footpaths left by my descent and the tears were flowing down my cheeks and freezing on them. It was already past midnight and the new day was May 24, the brightest of all the Bulgarian holidays for me!

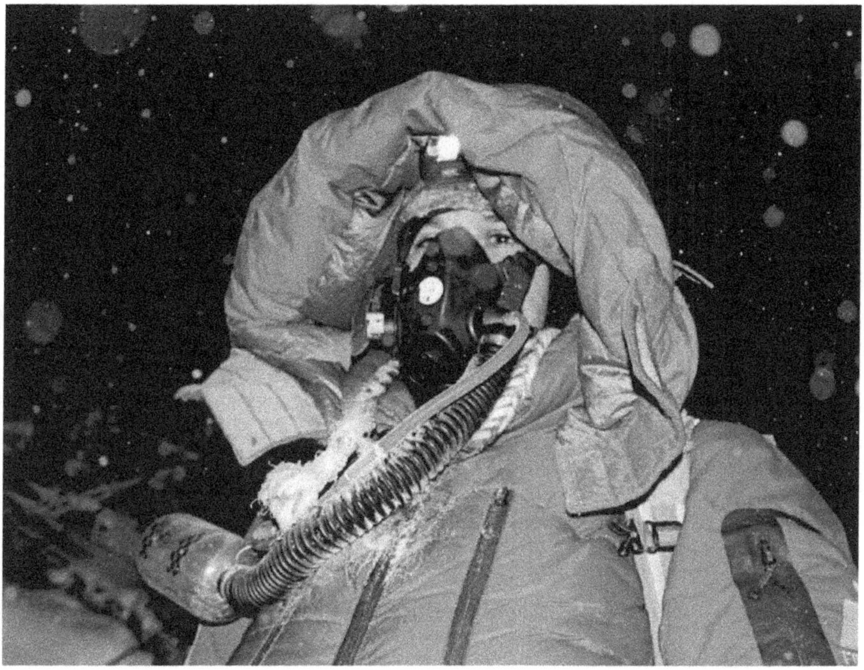

8450 metres where we wasted an hour in discussions.

DAY 50

00.00 on May 24, 2014

A few minutes later we caught up with David once again and passed him. I don't know whether it was because of the long and tense stand-off, or because of the discussion, fatigue or from nerves, but I could no longer walk as fast as before. We were only 10-15 metres in front of the Russians and they were following us. We passed through the same climbing places until we emerged onto the very edge and turned right towards the summit. We had to be very careful here, because there was an abyss to our left, on the Nepalese side. I walked ahead with the Sherpa and the others behind me. Something like a wall rose up in front of us and I saw the rope which leads up the rock face. I had no idea where to go because the snow was hiding the guide rope.

It was still dark, and visibility was severely reduced. I had set the head torch to low, so as not to waste the battery, because in this cold I did not know how long it would last. After about 20-30 minutes the snow stopped as if by order. The wind abated and the heavens were lit up with stars. We had reached Step One, about 8570 metres. At the beginning of this step, there's a little climbing required, following by strong pulling up using the Jumara. Here Gilgen took the lead. This situation became quite tense until we got to the first ladder. I didn't know precisely where we were going, since the guide rope was beneath the snow. We climbed up an aluminium ladder, and immediately after it there was a second one. It was slightly tilted to one side and tied only using ropes, so it moved from side to side. There were a lot of rope guide ropes hanging down. I was supposed to hang on to them and pull myself up. It wasn't easy, but this first step wasn't that difficult either. I pulled myself up using my muscles and made it past Step One. After Step One, Gilgen and I turned left at a suitable place to rest. We let the Russians and their Sherpas walk ahead to make a path in the snow, and we took advantage of that.

The Russians started in front of us, but walked no more than 100 metres before stopping supposedly to rest. They were hoping that we would overtake them again and continue to make a path for them. We had no choice. After resting, Gilgen and I went on up again. We reached Step Two, at 8620 metres. There was an aluminium ladder of about four or five metres in height, ending on a vertical rock, about one metre across. I climbed the ladder, and only at the upper end, I pulled myself up the guide rope to reach the top platform. We kept going on ahead with the others behind us. About 150 metres before Step Three, at 8,700 metres, I wanted to rest and eat something. We sat down, drank tea, ate some bars and watched two Russian pairs pass us. We got up after a while and continued on up.

Dawn was breaking, and only now at sunrise did I see where I was. Oooh, my God ... Where was I ... And there was not a sign of wind or fog. Step Three was nothing special

first a little climb, followed by a steep and long climb along a snowy and icy track, and a very steep slope. We overtook one Russian pair, and the other was about 30 metres in front of us. It was just here that the sun appeared. It was 4.45 and the most beautiful sunrise in my life! I kept looking back at the sunrise and wanted to take photographs, but Gilgen just grumbled that we didn't have much time. If we hadn't wasted an hour talking, we would have been on top by now, just as I had wanted to at sunrise.

The sun was fiery and dazzling. At this altitude, you can see the roundness of the Earth. The horizon is slightly curved at both ends. After a long ascent along this track, we turned right onto a traverse and walked along a flat section for about 200-300 metres until we reached a channel on the north side of the top. We set off along the channel. We climbed and pulled ourselves up with the Jumara. By this time we had already caught up with the Russian and his Sherpa. They were the only climbers in front of us.

After the channel we continued to the left, to the east. Then we turned sharply along the edge back towards the west in the direction of the summit. I signalled to Gilgen that we had to overtake them. I could move faster than them but the terrain wouldn't allow us to overtake them and they hadn't stopped.

For about 10-15 minutes the four of us walked one behind the other. Suddenly the Russian stopped, and I immediately moved my Jumara in front of his and saw snow ahead of us. I thought there was still some distance to go. However, I took only a couple of steps and realised that we are at the very top. This is where the guide rope ended. It was 5.50 am Nepalese time on May 24, 2014 and I was on the Roof of the World. The four of us stood there hugging each other.

The Roof of the World, Chomolungma peak, 8848 metres, 5.50 hours Nepalese time

I still couldn't believe I was on the top of Everest. The weather was beautiful. It was sunny and the wind was not as strong as I thought it would be. There was a westerly wind, but only two feet below, on the east side, there was no wind. What enormous joy and beauty! I had two video cameras and a stills camera which I had zipped away in the inside pockets of my down-filled suit across my chest. I realised as I ascended that the zip was frozen, but I decided to try and unfreeze it at the top and get them out. However, at the top, when I started trying to move the zip, I realized that it was completely frozen and wouldn't budge. Then Gilgen took out his camera and told me not to worry. He would take some pictures and let me have them. Condensation formed when I breathed through the mask, and the drops fell on the zip freezing it. That's where the problem had come from. The suit also had zips at the bottom, but they were under my seat. In order to open them, I would have to remove or loosen the harness which meant taking off my gloves. That was impossible to do at this altitude. I had heard of many cases climbers getting frostbitten fingers and hands while taking photographs on Everest or other high peaks. Gilgen pulled out his camera and started taking photographs.

The first flag on Mount Everest, 8848 metres, which I unfurled.

The official Vegan expedition flag "Everest North, 2014 Dr. Atanas Skatov"

The flag of the Municipality of Sliven on Mount Everest, 8848 metres

First I took out the flag which I had made for my son Vasko and asked him to take a picture of me holding it. Then I held up the expedition flag and the flag of Sliven Municipality and two other flags. Then he asked me to take off my goggles and my oxygen mask to take a picture of my face. I stood for about ten minutes without the oxygen mask on my face, but I didn't feel much difference. I was breathing normally, I guess it was the euphoria of being on the Roof of the World. Two metres to the west of us just below the summit, there were flags and prayer flags. There must have been more than two metres of new snow and so we were even higher than the top.

I put the mask back on again, because the wind was freezing my face. Apart from providing you with oxygen, the mask also protects you from the wind. I didn't give up my struggle with the zip. I eventually managed to pull one of the cameras out through the neck without undoing the zip, and took a panoramic video clip from the top. We had been at the top for about 30 minutes now, and Gilgen was anxious to descend. I didn't want to go down on this wonderful day and such a bright holiday for Bulgaria. As I filmed, Gilgen radioed the Advance Base Camp to tell them that we were at the summit. Most people when they get to the top, take a couple of pictures and hurried down, following the instructions of the expedition organisers. We welcomed all the Russians and one Pole and they left before we did. *My Sherpa Gilgen and me on Mount Everest, 8848 metres*

Mount Everest, 8848 metres without a mask.

On the way down, we met another Pole who often came to our camp and talked to our Poles. He didn't have a Sherpa and was walking alone.

The views from the top were amazing. There was visibility in all directions, more than 100 kilometres, I imagine. I could see Makalu, Lhotse, Shishapangma, Cho Oyu and countless other known and unknown peaks. I couldn't stop admiring the view. The Russian I had walked with to the top with were long gone.

On the way down from the top, after about fifteen metres, we stopped to change our oxygen cylinders. My Sherpa took the empty bottles because they got $50 for each returned bottle. Perhaps he was just being responsible and didn't want to pollute the environment. All along the way, there were discarded bottles, but the photographs of piles of rubbish and bottles I had seen were clearly from the Nepalese side of Everest.

The Nepalese usually sell 500 permits every year, while from the north, no more than 100-150 permits are sold, at least for now. These bottles and tents were minimal environmental pollution, when compared to the entire industry of the world and the lives of nearly 7.3 billion people on the planet. I don't want to dwell on the topic of environmental pollution by climbers. It's actually insignificant compared to industrial pollution, pollution from aircraft, ships, livestock breeding and so on. It's not mountaineering that pollutes the environment.

We changed our bottles, took out the camera again and started filming on the way down. I filmed almost all the way back down from the top. Gilgen constantly nagged at me that we were still at high altitude and every second counted. But what did I care, he'd been here nine times before and it was my first time. He was a very fit man with a difficult character, but no match for me. He didn't know me very well at first, but today we both got to know each other a lot better.

The descent was very fast, but in certain places more dangerous. Just a short distance before Step Two, we met David, who was really struggling and spitting blood. This was the maximum height he had reached in all seven of his attempts to climb Everest without oxygen. I stayed with him for a while and prayed fervently that he would get down safe and sound. We headed on down. He followed with his Sherpa. For David, the expedition was over. At Step Two, the ascent is easy, but the descent is more difficult. The ladder doesn't go above the rock platform and on the way back down you have to go in reverse. You have to crawl backwards on your stomach until you step on the ladder. This was the first time I felt a little scared during the expedition. If I missed the rung on the ladder, I didn't know if the guide rope would hold on to me and where I would land. We got through the Second Step, then the First Step and before noon we were in Camp 3.

Another fact I don't want to dwell on is that there were about 13-14 corpses on the way, some of them even just above Camp 3 itself. I didn't take any photographs of them. Respect needs to be shown for the dead, and they must be allowed to rest in peace on the eternal ice. I also saw the body of Hristo Hristov, the Bulgarian climber who remained on the mountain in 2004. I knew how the Bulgarians had been dressed in 2004 and I recognized him very easily. I stopped for a moment on both my ascent and descent, to pay tribute to this amazing boy because I realised what it was like to climb without oxygen. The difference can be fatal.

On the way down to Camp 3, about 8500 metres, North edge

Besides David, this year there were two others who planned to climb without oxygen, but none of them succeeded. There was no oxygen-free ascent of Everest in 2014. I regretted not trying, but Everest is still there. There's still time.

When we got back to the camp we were greeted by the other participants in the expedition. They had already heard from Gilgen and the Serdar that we had reached the top. We were also congratulated by other expeditions. We stayed in the camp for about two hours. I didn't feel tired, so Gilgen and I agreed to go down to the Advance Base Camp at 6,440 metres. At Camp 3 I called my parents on the satellite phone to tell them that I had climbed to the top and was in Camp 3. I also called another friend of mine, a journalist in Sliven, so that she could let everyone else know. I told her that I had used oxygen because the other Bulgarian climbers who managed the climb had also used oxygen. That was what they were interested in, although my mission was completely different and I didn't expect such people to understand what I was doing.

Climbers say that the moment you take a breath with an oxygen mask, it's not considered an oxygen-free ascent, but here I want to draw attention to the fact that the amount of oxygen used is also very important, for both mental and physical exertion. It's one thing to use 6, 7, 8 or 11 bottles, it's something else to use 5, and yet something completely different to use 3 or 4. Personally, I think that I could have used less oxygen, but this was my first time on such an expedition, at such an altitude. There were a lot of things I didn't know, and I couldn't have predicted how I would feel. I didn't want to take unnecessary risks. One day when I feel ready for it and it's a worthwhile cause, I might try an oxygen- free climb. There had to be a meaning in everything we do. More than 200 people have climbed Everest without oxygen, so it's been proven that it can be done. There's nothing new under the sun. Only the risk remains. A vegan has now climbed Everest. However, no vegan has yet done it without oxygen.

In Camp 3, Gilgen nor I felt like waiting while the ice melted to make water. We were tired and dehydrated. I knew how important it was to drink water, but at this altitude the ice melted very slowly. We took a risk, but fortunately there were no consequences. It was a good thing we didn't sweat much.

We found Kristiano and Richard in the camp. Kristiano explained to me that he hadn't felt well on their ascent yesterday. He didn't have the strength to walk and he decided to go back down. It wasn't because of the weather. I don't know why Richard had gone back down, but they had agreed that Kristiano would give his oxygen to Richard and he would try for the top for the second time tonight. Since they didn't have enough for them both to make the ascent, Kristiano would stay in the camp, where oxygen consumption was much lower, and Richard would make a second attempt and raise their sponsors' flags. Last year, Richard had been with another female client. He left her in Camp 3 and climbed to the top for the fourth time while she descended with her Sherpa. I heard that she was suing him for impropriety, and there may have been other circumstances.

My personal advice to all mountaineers and tourists is never to put their complete trust in professional mountaineer guides. You need to be very wary of them because they can quite easily abandon you on the way. On the other hand, these people do it for the money and don't let you decide what your body and spirit want. I know of such cases in Bulgaria as well. People have paid professional guides, only to be abandoned by them because of the climber's ego. He just has to get to the top and show that he is immortal and the greatest. That's enough advertising for this small, closed society. I saw for myself that the only person you should listen to in the mountains is yourself and you have judge your own abilities and the weather if that's possible.

Gilgen and I went down thirsty. We had climbed and descended with only half a litre of tea in my thermos. I told him to bring some water, but he didn't want to carry it. Who was the Sherpa and who was the client? So I was the only one with any liquid, and it wasn't enough for both of us. Of course, Gilgen was carrying the oxygen bottle I had replaced, and I was very grateful to him for that. But on the other hand, I had paid quite a hefty sum.

After Camp 3, the first climbers intent on attacking the summit that night began to appear. I was glad that I was one of the 15-20 people who climbed on May 24, because the next day on the way to Camp 3 we passed more than 100 climbers and Sherpas on their way up to the top. They included the Indians from my expedition who each had 7 bottles of oxygen. The lines of climbers walked slowly, and in places where we had to hold on to the guide rope for safety, we had to wait for them. I can't imagine what it was like that evening with all those people going to the top and how on earth they managed to pass each other. And imagine another 500 people from the Nepalese side. I would never do that to myself.

The weather was still good. The sky was clear and windless. Shortly after we returned to Camp 3, Kristiano went straight down with his Sherpa, I assumed they were going straight to the Advance Base Camp and would arrive there well before us. However, he gave up almost before he started, and spend all night and until noon the next day in Camp 3, resting in our tent. We caught up with him shortly before Camp 2. He said that he did not have the strength to walk and was astonished that I had been all the way to the top and still had the strength to walk so briskly. How could I tell him that over the last three years I had probably walked more kilometres than he had in his entire life. He compared himself to me and thought that since he considered himself a vegan, he really must be. Everest is not climbed physically but mentally.

On the way down, just before Camp 3, Gilgen and I stopped to rest by a small cave. Inside it lay a corpse covered with stones. Gilgen told me that he hadn't expected me to be so mentally resilient. "You've got a very good head," he told me. He couldn't believe that after descending 100 metres during our first attempt, I still wanted to go back up and that I had managed to overcome all the obstacles along the way.

At Camp 2 we stopped for me to collect my stick and have a rest. I didn't need to rest, but I stopped because of Gilgen, who was starting to get pains in his knees. After all, he was over 40 years old and had been working as a high altitude porter since the age of 16. His joints must have been really worn out from the heavy weights. At Camp 2 we overtook Kristiano and we never saw him again that day.

Between Camp 2 and Camp 1 we took more frequent breaks, and at Camp 1 the Chinese gave us tea and water and we stayed there to pack. I had a down jacket, an inflatable bed roll and some small things. I packed my rucksack again. Somewhere between Camp 1 and 2 I ran out of oxygen and didn't use any more. I could have used another full bottle if I wanted to, but I didn't bother. Victor and Alex, as well as their Sherpas, had given up, and so there were 18 bottles left over. The stick I picked up at Camp 2, I promptly forgot at Camp 1. It was only when I descended the wall and picked up my second stick that I realised I had forgotten it in front of the Chinese tent.

Going down North Col this time was very difficult. I had been on my feet for 20 hours and I was exhausted by this time. I had the strength to walk, but the descent of the wall required other technical skills, and by this time I was already carrying a heavy rucksack. Gilgen abandoned me at the top and let himself down quickly, and I waited for him all day long because of his painful knees. The entire descent, including the wall, has to be done with only a single carabineer and you have to control everything yourself. I started to descend, but my legs couldn't take the strain and what with the weight of my rucksack as well, so I decided to use the eight-ring rope descender. It was only taking up room in my pack and I hadn't used it yet. So I attached myself to the eight-ring, but the rope guide ropes were so tightly stretched that it barely worked. I too frequent rests, fell, got up, even hurt myself, but eventually I managed to get down to the base of the wall, where there was a kitchen boy with some warm juice waiting for us. I don't normally drink powdered juice, but this time I was very glad of it.

We spent maybe half an hour at the base of the wall before I headed back down to Advance Base Camp. I crossed the glacier and reached the spot where I took off my crampons and climbing seat, and finally only the most difficult few metres to the camp were left. Gilgen and I arrived at the camp shortly before dark. We were greeted warmly with noisy applause and congratulations. I forgot to mention that on the way down between Camp 3 and Camp 2, we must have passed more than 100 climbers who all congratulated me and looked at me with respect and admiration. I don't know how they knew that I had succeeded in getting to the top, because there were others - like Kristiano, for example, who had failed on May 24.

And so, on May 24, 2014, after climbing Mount Chomolungma, I succeeded in getting down to Advance Base Camp at 6440 metres. No one had managed that apart from me and my Sherpa that season. The same day, David managed to get down to Camp 2, and Kristiano from Camp 3 to Camp 1 with his Sherpa. Neither of them had made it to the top. The other Sherpas at Advanced Base Camp told me that they had seen other people come straight down from the top to the Advance Camp, but they all looked really exhausted and in bad shape, while I looked perfectly normal, not like someone who had just descended from the Roof of the World. Well, they might just be exaggerating so that I would give them some equipment or money.

Gilgen and the other Sherpas had dinner, and I was so tired I could have fallen asleep right where I was sitting. One of the Sherpas offered to take my rucksack and equipment back to the tent. I had no idea that he actually wanted to steal my gloves. He helped me with my rucksack, although I could have carried it ten metres to the tent. The moment I entered the tent, I instantly fell asleep, even though I was at 6440 metres.

Tibet photographed from 8560 metres, Changtse Peak, Camp 2 and Camp 1

DAY 51

May 25 2014

I don't know exactly when I woke up, but the sun had warmed the tent so much that it must have been 20 degrees inside and really pleasant. I was puffy and dehydrated. The first thing I noticed in the light was that the gloves I wore under my big mittens were missing. They weren't expensive, I bought them from Kathmandu for $15 before the expedition, but I'm very fond of my equipment. I immediately the Sherpa who offered to help me and had supposedly brought them to my tent. So I got up and stretched, then went to the dining tent to see if they were there, and to have some to eat. Just as I suspected - that thieving Sherpa must have thought that I would be too exhausted after descending from the top to remember anything. I didn't say a word to him and waited to see what would happen.

The weather was beautiful and I wondered whether to pack my bags and go down to Base Camp, or stay here for another night. I spoke to the Serdar and he confirmed that the yaks would be coming on May 29 to take everything down, and that we would be leaving Base Camp for Kathmandu on May 30 or 31. That would be no problem, since my plane ticket was for the third of June from Kathmandu to Istanbul.

For two days and two nights, the ice on my hat wouldn't melt.

I decided to stay at ABC for another day and go down the next day. I told Gilgen about my plan, he had to stay until the 29th as well to pack for the expedition. I asked him to give me the memory card out of his camera so that I could download the photos on some laptop and even send some to Bulgaria. Gilgen looked at me with a guilty expression and told me that he would give me the pictures in Kathmandu. There was something funny going on, I said to myself. I have a very strong sense of intuition, especially then. We might not even see each other in Kathmandu, if I leave earlier. I told him that even if I did leave earlier, I would leave the memory stick on the chef's camera or someone else's camera. I also said that I would give him 16 gigabytes of memory for his camera and my down-filled suit as well. I had asked him before what he needed and he asked for my suit, because his was very old and not a branded one. He didn't even agree to give me the memory card in return for my overalls. Then I realized that it was all about money. I didn't think Gilgen was that sort of person. He wasn't the sort to ask for money, he had never mentioned it before. It's possible that he might have expected some additional money, which might even have been why he tried to prevent me from getting to the top. Serdar Mingma who was related to Gilgen's wife, had told him he could make money from the photos. He didn't name a specific amount, but the fact that he didn't give me them and wanted to meet me in Kathmandu to negotiate, made it quite clear in my mind that it was about money.

I lost my temper and went to Mingma. I looked him straight in the eyes and told him that what he was doing was shameful and disloyal. I told him I knew the other Sherpa had stolen my gloves the day before. The other Sherpa was right next to him and I told him directly in the eyes to give me back my gloves, or I would call the Base Camp police. Everyone ganged up against me. Apparently no one had ever stood up to them like that before. This caused a lot of tension and I didn't want to stay in the Advance Camp any longer, but it was already afternoon and I didn't want to go to Base Camp.

Kristiano and David arrived that evening with their Sherpas. At dinner, I told Kristiano what was going on, not that he cared, but I wanted him to know. So the afternoon was spent quarrelling with the ungrateful Sherpas who think only of money. They see us tourists only as a source of money, and nothing else. Of course, they're not all thieves like the one who stole my gloves. I'm sure that Gilgen would never take anything from anyone. He was honest but dependent on Mingma. The next day he even told me that Mingma and Dava, the manager of the Kathmandu company, would not allow him to give me the pictures.

I was furious when I went to bed that evening. I couldn't care less about my photographs. I had got to the top of Everest, I had seen and experienced everything. That's the reason I had scaled the mountain, not for the photographs.

DAY 52

May 26 2014

The forecast was for good weather only on the May 24 and 25. That night the window closed, heavy snow began to fall and the wind increased. In the morning everything was covered by 50 centimetres of new snow and it was still snowing. It was a good job I had descended from North Col the day before. I regretted that I hadn't left for Base Camp the day before. Kristiano had decided to wait for Richard and go down together. However, I told him that the weather was going to get worse and he would be better coming down with me. Which is what we did. I asked Gilgen for the photographs one last time. I offering him my down-filled suit, but he refused saying that his managers wouldn't allow it. So I gave Kristiano my suit to put it in his luggage. I didn't have much room in my duffel bag, and I had already locked other bag and was ready to go down. I had my last argument with the Sherpa rogues, and Kristiano and I headed on down.

We were lucky that there were plenty of yaks that days going down, they showed us the way and made a path through the snow. Even though it would have been my eighth trip down this road, I don't think I would have been able to find it in the snow. There were fissures, lakes, rivers that needed to be crossed, and everything was hidden by the snow and fog. Kristiano walked slowly, but I waited. I was glad of my Batura boots for the descent. The three-season boots I used between Base and the Advance Base Camp weren't suitable for the snow and terrain today. One of the yaks has fallen through the ice and it was being unloaded so that they could pull it out. The snow was really heavy. I had never imagined it could happen at this time of year. It was too early for the monsoon season, and these monsoon snows on May 26 were one or two weeks earlier than normal.

We slowly reached the Intermediate Camp. All there was left was one of the organiser's tents, with a couple of Tibetans inside. The whole tent was sodden and leaking. We went inside to warm up and have a cup of tea. I gave the boys a vegan bar each. We set off again and took care to follow the yaks. It only took ten minutes for their tracks to fill with snow, and there was no trace of where they had passed. The descent to Base Camp was very difficult. It took us almost a whole day.

Base camp, 5200 metres

I was so angry about the photos and my gloves that had been stolen, that as soon as I got to Base Camp, I went to the officer and told him the whole story. I didn't pass over the fact that Serdar Mingma was up to his tricks was selling illegal things, and that I wanted to tell the police about my stolen gloves. The officer was taken aback. He explained to me diplomatically that if I called the police, it would be very difficult for everyone. We would all have to write a lot of statements, and my company would lose its license in China and wouldn't be able to come back here. He said he would talk to Mingma and sort things out. He even offered me a ride to Zangma on May 28. There would be a jeep that I could travel on for free. I knew it cost $800, and another $500 to drop off my luggage before May 29. They were prepared to do me a really big favour, so that I could leave as soon as possible, and not look for justice; another hobby of mine.

Everything sounded good. When I looked at the weather, I didn't see what else there was to do, even at Base Camp, 5,200 metres, where there was already 40 cm of snow. I had had enough of everything already.

David joined us at dinner. He had come down after us, and he didn't look well at all. I hope he recovered quickly. Personally, I already felt restored and in the mood to fight for my rights.

FROM BASE CAMP TO KATHMANDU, ISTANBUL AND SLIVEN

Day 53 to day 55

DAY 53

May 27 2014

In the morning at Base Camp there was more than 50cm of snow! The snow was quite amazing. I had never imagined that it could snow so much. In all the fifty days since I had been here, no more than five inches of snow had fallen. And now it was snowing so heavily. It was a good thing we had descended the previous day. I met the officer again. He said that my luggage was already on its way with the yaks to Base Camp and that I was leaving for Kathmandu the next morning. I really wanted to leave and I couldn't really care less any more about the photos, the gloves, or who stole or who lied.

I spent the day in the dining tent. I didn't have any luggage to pack, since I had left it all at the ABC and it was already on its way down. All I had left at Base Camp was a rucksack with summer clothes and my sleeping bag that reeked of cigarettes. Nothing special happened. It didn't stop snowing all day long and it was quite thick underfoot. Richard turned up at dinner, frozen and wet through. He said that if it hadn't been for yaks, he wouldn't have been able to make it down to Base camp. Then to my utter surprise, Mingma and Gilgen appeared. Clearly the officer had ordered them to come down to hand over the photographs, because I had threatened to go to the police. Gilgen didn't enter the tent, but went straight to bed. We agreed that we'd talk in the morning, because it was too late now. My luggage by now was in the Chinese camp next door. I could pick it up in the morning and leave.

I packed my things and went to bed for the last night at Base Camp. Things had turned very unpleasant after all those unique experiences and positive emotions at the summit of Everest.

Base camp

DAY 54

May 28, 2014

It snowed all night long and by morning it was almost level with my tent, about 80 centimetres deep. I spent all night shaking the snow off the tent, so that I wouldn't be trapped in it when morning came. The jeep came to pick us up early. David and Adina had also paid to leave earlier. Not only did David have the most expensive expedition with all sorts of additional extras, but he continued to add to the final bill even now. The jeep barely reached the camp when Mingma and Gilgen told me they would give me the pictures, but in return for the down-filled suit I had bought in Kathmandu at Mingma's shop for $400. We had agreed when I bought it that if I returned it to him after the expedition, he would refund me $200. So it was all about those $200. Then I explained that I had given my suit to Kristiano the day before to put in his luggage for Base Camp because I had no more room. Kristiano confirmed that my suit was with his luggage and that when it was taken down to Base camp, he would give it Gilgen. They agreed and gave me the photos. With the space of five minutes literally, Kristiano transferred them to one of my flash drives.

I asked Mingma about the certificate issued by the Chinese Tibetan Mountain Service to everyone who has successfully climbed the peak. Mingma replied that the Chinese at Base Camp had run out of paper, and that only the Russians and Swiss would be getting their certificates here and now. Mine and those of the other participants in our expedition would be sent in the post. I didn't know whether to believe him or not, but I had had enough of it all, and I hadn't climbed Everest just for a piece of paper. I just couldn't be bothered to call the officer again and ask him for the certificate. A month after I got back to Bulgaria, I received the original certificate from the Chinese-Tibetan Mountaineer Service by post. I stated that I had successfully climbed the peak with a date and time. David, Adina, and I got in the jeep with the cook who also wanted to go to Kathmandu. David and Adina expressed their annoyance that they were in a hurry for their flight the next day, and I was slowing them down. The plan was to be in Kathmandu today.

Everest Base Camp

Yaks of the Base Camp, 5200 metres

We got off to a good start, but there was over 60 centimetres of snow on the road and it was still falling heavily. The driver couldn't see past the end of his nose, as if he was driving in fog. In certain sections the road from Base Camp narrows and it was extremely dangerous to travel with no visibility. Everything around us was white as milk. The driver set off and began to pray aloud. The cook was in the front and the three of us were in the back. Not more than two or three kilometres from Base Camp and about the same distance from the T-shop, we heard a loud metallic bang, and the left side of the jeep was hanging in mid air. What had happened this time? Very carefully we got out of the jeep only to see that the left wheel was hanging in mid air over an unsupported bridge. If the driver had been driving a little faster, the entire vehicle would have fallen into the ravine. It looked pretty serious. It was only to be expected in this snow with zero visibility. We started wondering about what to do. David and Adina walked down to the T-shop and showed little interest in what was happening to the jeep or whether we would make it back. The driver called the officer for reinforcements. It was very cold and snowing heavily. We got out the jacks and unloaded our luggage. The problem was that the rear left wheel was almost entire hanging in the air, while half the front axle was hanging over the other side of the bridge. The entire jeep was lying on its chassis. We could see that the suspension bars were bent. I didn't believe we were going to make it out of here today. I really hoped they would send another car to pick us up.

The jeep went off the road onto an unsupported bridge, 5,100 metres

About 20-30 minutes had passed when the officer arrived with a group of other people. The yakmen with their herds of yaks also began to arrive. Instead of leaving for Advance Base Camp to pick up the expedition luggage, the yaks were stopping work because of the snow.

I later found out that my luggage was the last to be brought down for the next ten days. I was in luck that I could get my luggage and leave on time. A group of about 15 people along with the officer gathered. Everyone wondered about how to get the car back on the road. It was a very heavy jeep. They started trying to lift it, but to no avail. I also did my bit to help, and then I took pictures with the camera. I filmed the whole rescue operation on my video camera. We started lifting the jeep on the jack and then placing large rock beneath it. Then we raised it some more and placed more rocks, eventually rocking it back onto the road. This gave us some hope and after about an hour or so, millimetre by millimetre we got the car back onto the road. It took a lot of hard work and effort. Now, however, we had to make sure everything was all right and whether the engine would start.

We got in and it started first time. This time, two yakmen who knew the road like the back of their hands, walked in front of the jeep to show us where to drive so we wouldn't fall off the road again. All the yak herds were coming back down. David and Adina were in such a hurry in the morning and couldn't care less about my problems with the photographs. The accident took us exactly 4 and a half hours. Not to mention that we had to drive down to the T-shop at 5-6 km per hour. It was noon by the time we got there. We started looking for the Hungarians who were sitting in a tavern having lunch. We loaded up again and headed for the town of Tingri. For about 30-40 km after the T-shop the road was still deep in snow. There were lots of vehicles tuck in the snow drifts and everyone was moving very slowly. Our driver overtook all of them and by the time the snow ended, we were alone. I was happy to be on my way home. My flight to Bulgaria was in five days' time. However, I decided that if I managed to get to Kathmandu earlier, I would catch the first flight to Istanbul.

That evening we reached the border at Zangmu. I had already slept in their luxury hotel, with its rich menu of good food and abundance of fruit and vegetables. Once again I ordered the combined salad with fruits and vegetables and rice with dal and spices. I really love Nepalese cuisine. My first hot shower after reaching the top. I had read somewhere that the first shower after such an expedition was something special. Well, it didn't feel like that. My head was already in Bulgaria and all the new challenges that were waiting for me.

DAY 54

May 29 2014

In the morning, after breakfast, the four of us took a taxi to the border about 5-6 km away down a steep road. The Chinese border opens at 10.00 and we were right on time, but they decided to open it later today. We were followed by Kobler and the Seven Summits Club. I almost felt as if I was on expensive $ 65,000 Everest expedition. I chatted to my colleagues as we queued and we exchanged addresses and telephone numbers.

They opened the border, started checking luggage and filling out forms. As always, all the luggage was being carried by Nepalese women. On the other side of the bridge, already in Nepal, our company's minibus was waiting for us and we loaded up our luggage for Kathmandu. On the way we stopped for lunch. I called my sister on the satellite phone to tell her that I would be in Kathmandu in two hours' time. I asked her to book me on the first possible flight to Istanbul. I wanted to leave straight away even though I had three more nights in Kathmandu provided by the company.

At the China Nepal border, the luggage is carried by Nepalese women.

By the time I arrived in Kathmandu, my sister had arranged a flight that evening to Istanbul via Doha. At 14.00 the minibus dropped me off at my hotel in Kathmandu. My flight was at 19.30. I had two hours to shop for gifts, souvenirs, to return some brand new crampons to Mingma's shop. I had brought them before the expedition as a backup. They would refund me $100 if they were unopened. And I had paid 150 for them.

I just left my luggage at the hotel and went straight out to look for what I needed. It took me two hours to find what I needed and went back to the hotel for dinner before I left. I had 30 minutes for dinner before I was to be picked up to go to the airport. A journalist from Elizabeth Holly's agency was waiting for me at the hotel, the same one who had interviewed me before the expedition. This time it was a young boy, an American, who diligently filled out the questionnaire while I had my dinner. He wrote down everything I told him.

The dinner was delicious - this time a speciality with chickpeas. I literally only had time to go up to my room and pick up my luggage. The car to take me to the airport was already waiting for me. I didn't even have time to take a shower or rest on my bed for five minutes.

When I got to the airport, I realised I had 40 kg of luggage, but only 30 kg allowance. I would have to pay for the rest as excess luggage at ten dollars per kilogramme. I had decided to pay for it, if I had to. The boy at the counter asked me where I had come from. I told him I had climbed Sagarmatha a few days earlier (that's the name of the peak in Nepal). Then he shook meby the hand and called his manager on the phone. An older gentleman appeared and he also began to congratulate me. He told me that I wouldn't have to pay anything and that it was an honour for them to shake my hand. I was a little surprised. A lot of people had climbed Everest, but after the recent tragedy, I was the first climber they had seen this year who had reached the top. So there still are decent people.

I got on the plane and all I wanted to do was to watch my favourite film and enjoy the flight and the food. Qatar Airlines is probably the best airline when it comes to their food and service. As I have already said, their planes are new, modern and reliable.

At around midnight I landed in the amazing airport of Doha. I spent an hour looking for the cubicle where I had slept two months previously but I didn't find it. It was like looking for a needle in a haystack in such a huge airport. I found a different one, but I couldn't sleep.

DAY 55

May 30 2014

I spent the night at Doha airport, where I slept fitfully. I spent most of my time on the computers surfing the net. Nobody in Bulgaria knew when I was due to arrive, except my closest friends and family. I didn't want anyone to meet me, no television crews or journalists. There was interest from the media, but I had categorically turned them down. I don't think that I had achieved that much. All I had done was to test a certain diet in combination with high-altitude tourism or as some might call it high-altitude mountaineering. If I can one day contribute in some way to protecting the environment, and being a positive influence people, then the project would have been worth it.

In the morning I took a short walk around the airport before boarding the plane for the big city of Istanbul.

Slightly behind schedule, we landed in the metropolis between Europe and Asia. Only my closest friends and family were there to welcome me. My friend Kaloyan had organized the transport. I was very happy to see them all. It doesn't take long to get from Istanbul to Sliven, especially at weekends when there's not much traffic. So by May 30 I was in back in my hometown beneath the Blue Rocks.

As we parked in front of the apartment block, I was surprised by the sound of the typical Bulgarian bagpipes and people with bouquets of flowers. It initially thought it was a neighbour's wedding or something. I took a second look and saw familiar faces holding flowers, flags and bagpipes. I was so overjoyed at their surprise welcome. I didn't really want anyone to meet me but I was very happy. We danced a traditional circle dance and drank rakiya brandy. A lot of people had come out to congratulate me. Thank you very much, dear friends, you touched me very much!

Well, that's how my adventure with the Mother Goddess ended. I felt wonderful, healthy, filled with love, emotions and intense experiences. I had committed every day and hour of this expedition to my memory and these memories bring me joy and positive emotions. But there was still a sense of anxiety... I still didn't have a plane ticket for the next destination...

To be continued....

THE BALANCE SHEET

The Everest expedition left a deep mark on my life. These 55 days were filled with unforgettable moments, strong feelings, emotions, amazing views, intense cold and hardships. I am grateful that I had the incredible chance to participate in such an adventure. It was part of a grandiose project to find solutions to feed our race, save the lives of animals and protect the environment.

Most importantly, my ascent of Everest proved that one can live a quite normal life without consuming animal-based food, and not only that - the body and psyche can withstand excessive loads. I also proved that anything is possible and every dream can come true.

Although my supplementary food did not arrive at Base Camp, I didn't switch to a vegetarian diet. In fact I spent almost two months living on a diet of only potatoes, rice and spaghetti as a staple food, and some local vegetables at an altitude of 5,200 to 8,848 metres above sea level. In this way I proved to myself that protein is not that important for a mature organism and can be consumed in much smaller quantities, even in cases of extreme physical load.

During this expedition I acquired extremely important knowledge and skills in high- altitude mountaineering. I learned how to survive and take care of myself and my companions.

From a psychological point of view, the results I achieved are of a very high level and it would be extremely difficult to share and explain a non-psychologist like me. Like many other peaks, climbing Everest is more of a psychological achievement. You have to have a healthy psyche, purpose and perseverance. You need to believe firmly in your success, be focused all the time and to give your best. In particular after Camp 1 at 7100 metres, you have to take care with every single step you take on your way to the top and assess the whole situation. One wrong step or wrong decision can cost you not only the failure of the expedition, but also your own life.

One very important quality I worked upon during this expedition was patience. Patience is a basic principle when you are making an important decision, both in extreme and normal conditions.

I have to mention the fact that Kristiano from Poland who consumed animal-based food products in abundance during the entire expedition, failed to reach 8,400 metres above sea level with six bottles of oxygen. It was a pity that he claimed to be a vegan. The Mother Goddess didn't allow him to the top.

I feel very sorry for David that he failed to reach the top again without oxygen. However, I think he made a lot of errors during his acclimatization which ultimately cost him the project. The most important thing is that he came down alive and well.

On the other hand, saw with my own eyes how difficult an oxygen-free ascent of Everest is. If one day I decide to climb Everest without oxygen, I know what I need to do. However, that has nothing to do with the decision of the Goddess - she is the one who decides whether to allow you to the top and come back alive and well.

FUTURE PLANS

One area is quite definite. I want to test the bounds of veganism and see if it is a healthy option for humans. I want to disseminate this information in order to reduce and even stop the breeding of animals for food.

I have many dreams and projects in mind. A year has passed since I climbed Everest. In 2014 I managed to climb two more continental peaks - Australia and Oceania, and Antarctica. I will soon be leaving for Alaska for the last peak of this project. Unfortunately, I have not been unable to find many supporters to enable me to publish this book and let more people know what I encountered during my expedition to the Roof of the World. I hope very much that the book will soon become a fact. Then why not my own film about Everest.

Despite the many challenges ahead, my next project will focus on the highest peaks on our planet. These are fourteen 8000 metre giants of the planet (14 x 8000), also called the Himalayan crown. I already have a name for my second project - "14 x 8000 x Vegan". You can find more about it on my website

If I can manage to accomplish it, nothing will be able to disprove veganism as a suitable way to feed the human race. However, all these expeditions require a certain amount of luck. It's not only important how well you have trained and how good you are, but the weather and other circumstances.

On April 25, 2015, Nepal was swept away by a devastating

earthquake of magnitude 8 on the Richter scale. More than 8,000 people were reported killed and at Everest Base Camp and more than 20 people were killed and 50 injured following the tremor and avalanche. The Nepalese government closed Mount Everest again for climbing, as it did in 2014. The same people who were unable to climb Everest the previous year, were stopped from doing so again. I don't want to comment on the number of victims. So no matter how physically and mentally trained and prepared you are, climbing a peak like Everest depends mainly on the weather and many other circumstances that no one can change.

China also closed the Northern approaches to Everest during the pre-monsoon period. Thus the 2015 season was closed.

For me, the future lies in the transformation of animal husbandry into crop production, horticulture, and fruit growing. I want to see the replacement of as much agricultural land as possible used for animal feed with agricultural land for human consumption of plant- based food. I also want to see a project for forestation in areas where forest trees have been felled for timber. We need to return to nature and live as naturally as possible. This must be the main mission of our generation and the generations to follow. Animal husbandry is detrimental not only to the environment due to pollution, but also to the morals and conscience of mankind, their karma, soul and psyche.

Let everyone judge for themselves what they want to achieve in this life and what they can give of themselves to enable mankind to live in a better world.

The newest achievement - the first vegan to climb the Soul of the Mountain - Mount Manaslu, 8165 metres on 1.10. 2015.

DEAR READER

Dear reader,

Sincere thanks for reading my book and reaching to its end. I do hope wholeheartedly that you have enjoyed reading it. This is the first edition and as such there would possibly be errors in the text. If you happened to find any errors please email george@atanasskatov.com. Those of you who send an email with errors to correct will receive an email next time I publish my other books to download a free ebook copy. From the bottom of my heart I am appealing to you to share your thoughts on the book by leaving a book review. Those of you who write a review and send back a proof of it to george@atanasskatov.com will receive my next ebook for free. I have other six in the pipline. To follow me and stay in touch, my social media are: Facebook -Dr. Atanas Skatov, my Twitter Dr Atanas Skatov (@DrSkatov) and my Instagram (@at.skatov). To subscribe to my newsletter, please email "subscribe" to team@atanasskatov.com.

To support my cause or stay updated with my project 14x8000xVegan you can check my website and buy from our branded and organic cotton products or donate at https://drskatov.com/ Please see some of our branded further products below

Sincere thanks and kindest regards,

Dr. Atanas Skatov.

Documentary

The documentary can be seen on YouTube - THE SKATOV EXPERIMENT or following the link here: t.ly/2bd9

Some of my branded organic products

www.drskatov.com

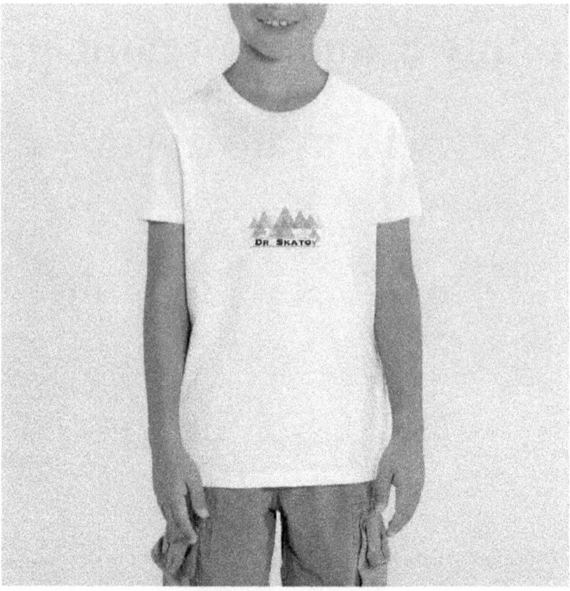
DR SKATOV

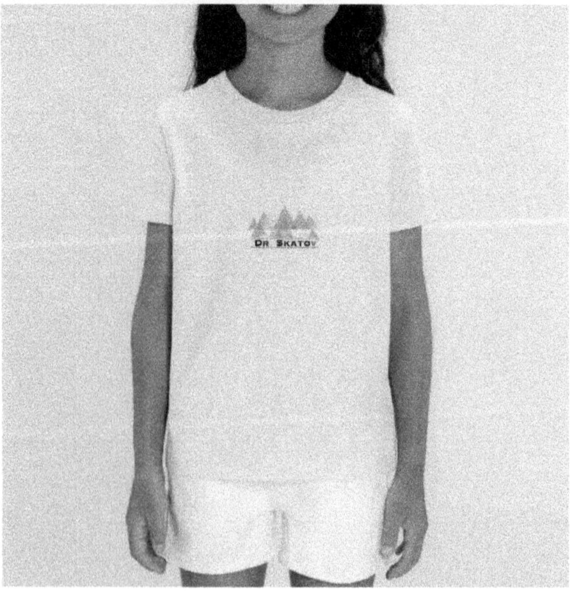
DR SKATOV

Other products

Find other products on www.drskatov.com

TIBETAN FACES

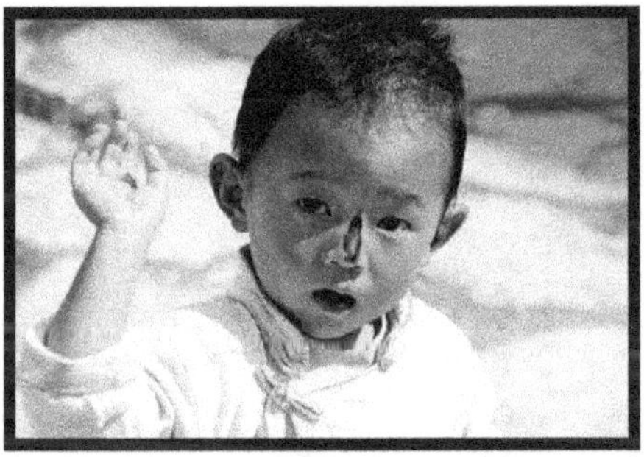

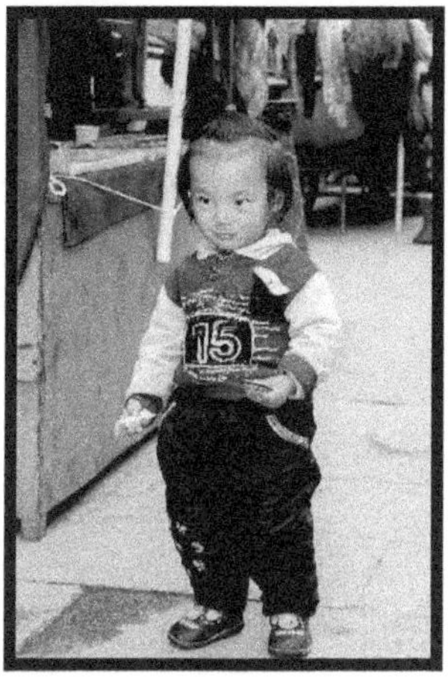

GLOSSARY

"IRON MAN" - triathlon competition with running - 42, 2 kilometres, cycling - 180 kilometres and swimming - 5 kilometres.

VEGETARIAN - a person who does not eat meat (some don't eat fish). VEGAN - a person who does not consume food of animal origin.

GEORGE HERBERT LEE MALLORY (June 18, 1886 - June 8 or 9, 1924) was an

English mountaineer who participated in the first three British expeditions to Mount Everest in the early 1920s.

JUMARA (ascender grip) - a device in climbing used by climbers to pull themselves up and self-locking when moving backwards.

ARTIFICIAL OXYGEN - iron bottles with a capacity of 4 litres of compressed oxygen.

GUIDE ROPE (PARAPET) - a taut rope that serves as a safety feature during the climb.

PASSAGE - a certain section of the route, especially in mountaineering ABC - Advances Base Camp, - 6400 metres RAPEL - roped descent using a device resembling the figure 8.

SATURATION - the oxygen content in the blood. SERDAR - the leader of the Sherpas and the expedition.

SARAC - years of accumulated snow with nothing below, but looks solid. Usually located high above the walker and may fall unexpectedly.

SUMMIT BONUS - a cash premium for reaching the top, received by the Sherpa - a high-altitude bearer and climb partner

HEAD TORCH - light source attached to the forehead.

CHOMOLUNGMA - the Tibetan name of Mount Everest, means

The First Vegan on Everest..

Sherpa (sher - east and pa - people) - a nation in Nepal. The main occupation of the Sherpas is to work as high-altitude porters in the Himalayas.

SEVEN SUMMITS - ascent of the highest peaks in the seven continents

Dr Atanas Skatov

www.ingramcontent.com/pod-product-compliance
Lightning Source LLC
Chambersburg PA
CBHW021219090426
42740CB00006B/290